THE AFRICAN & MIDDLE EASTERN —WORLD— 600–1500

STUDENT STUDY GUIDE

OXFORD
UNIVERSITY PRESS

Oxford University Press, Inc., publishes works that
further Oxford University's objective of excellence
in research, scholarship, and education.

Oxford   New York
Auckland   Cape Town   Dar es Salaam   Hong Kong   Karachi
Kuala Lumpur   Madrid   Melbourne   Mexico City   Nairobi
New Delhi   Shanghai   Taipei   Toronto

With offices in
Argentina   Austria   Brazil   Chile   Czech Republic   France   Greece
Guatemala   Hungary   Italy   Japan   Poland   Portugal   Singapore
South Korea   Switzerland   Thailand   Turkey   Ukraine   Vietnam

Copyright © 2005 by Oxford University Press, Inc.

Published by Oxford University Press, Inc.
198 Madison Avenue, New York, NY 10016
www.oup.com

Oxford is a registered trademark of Oxford University Press

All rights reserved. No part of this publication may be reproduced,
stored in a retrieval system, or transmitted in any form or by any means,
electronic, mechanical, photocopying, recording, or otherwise,
without the prior permission of Oxford University Press.

ISBN 978-0-19-522260-9 (California edition)   ISBN 978-0-19-522338-5

Writer: Erin Cleary
Editor: Lelia Mander
Project Director: Jacqueline A. Ball
Education Consultant: Diane L. Brooks, Ed.D.
Design: designlabnyc

Casper Grathwohl, Publisher

Printed in the United States of America
on acid-free paper

Dear Parents, Guardians, and Students:

This study guide has been created to increase student enjoyment and understanding of *The African & Middle Eastern World, 600–1500*. It has been developed to help students access the text. As they do so, they can learn history and the social sciences and improve reading, language arts, and study skills.

The study guide offers a wide variety of interactive exercises to support every chapter. Parents or other family members can participate in activities labeled "With a Parent or Partner." Adults can help in other ways, too. One important way is to encourage students to create and use a history journal as they work through the exercises in the guide. The journal can simply be an off-the-shelf notebook or three-ring binder used only for this purpose. Some students might like to customize their journals with markers, colored paper, drawings, or computer graphics. No matter what it looks like, a journal is a student's very own place to organize thoughts, practice writing, and make notes on important information. It will serve as a personal report of ongoing progress that your child's teacher can evaluate regularly. When completed, it will be a source of satisfaction and accomplishment for your child.

Sincerely,

Casper Grathwohl
Publisher

This book belongs to:

_____

CONTENTS

How to Use the Student Study Guides to *The Medieval & Early Modern World*   6

Graphic Organizers   8

Reports and Special Projects   10

Chapter 1   11
Camels, Caravans, and the Ka'ba: The Arabian Peninsula Around 600
Traders from the east and west made long, dangerous trips across the desert to exchange goods in Mecca.

Chapter 2   15
The Messenger of Allah: Muhammad and the Beginning of Islam
The prophet Muhammad brought many polytheistic people of Arabia together under the belief in one God. This monotheistic religion was called Islam.

Chapter 3   19
The Sword of Allah: The Islamic Expansion
The Islamic leaders after Muhammad helped to spread Islamic rule beyond the Arabian Peninsula, across northern Africa and into Spain.

Chapter 4   23
Managing the Empire: Islam Grows into an Empire of Faith
Islamic leaders could not decide on a clear successor to Umar, and eventually factions developed within the Muslim communities.

Chapter 5   27
The House of Islam: The First Worldwide Civilization
During the Abbasid caliphate, the Muslim Empire grew rapidly and became an important center for trade.

Chapter 6   31
Living by the Rules: Ulama and Philosophers
Early Muslims developed ways of interpreting the Quran and teachings of Muhammad to determine how they were supposed to live.

Chapter 7   35
Houses of Wisdom: Islamic Arts and Sciences
The Muslim world made important contributions to the fields of art and science. Muslim thinkers and artists have influenced scientists and philosophers throughout history.

Chapter 8   39
Now It's Istanbul, Not Constantinople: The Ottoman Empire
Ottoman leaders and their armies successfully expanded the Ottoman Empire throughout the Balkan Peninsula and to Europe.

Chapter 9   43
Where Gold Grows as Carrots Do: Ghana and the African Grasslands
The kingdom of Ghana, located in the grasslands of West Africa, prospered from trade with desert caravans. Berbers introduced Islam to the Ghana leadership, and eventually the Almoravids, a group of Sunni Muslims, converted the kingdom by force and brought about its decline.

Chapter 10   47
Saddlebags Stuffed with Gold: The Empires of Mali and Songhay
Two rich and powerful kingdoms, first Mali and then Songhay, emerged from Ghana starting in 1235. Although the leaders were Muslims, the people retained their traditional religious practices and beliefs in the African spirits. Internal rivalries and warfare with other nations led to Songhay's decline in the 16th century.

Chapter 11   51
Onis and Obas: The Forest Kings of West Africa
The Yoruba people lived in and around the trading center of Ifé, where traders came with goods such as ivory and kola nuts from the forests. The Yoruba kings, called the Oni, were thought to be divine according to ancient tradition. Beautiful bronze and brass sculptures were made to honor the kings, or Obas, of neighboring Benin.

Chapter 12   55
There's Treasure in Those Hills!: Great Zimbabwe and the Shona of Southern Africa
The civilizations of southeastern Africa first evolved from Bantu-speaking peoples. Over time they gave rise to the prosperous trading centers of Mapungubwe and Great Zimbabwe. After these cities went into decline, the kingdom of Mwenemutapa took over trade in the region, which was overrun by Portugal in the 1600s.

Chapter 13   59
The Empire's Giraffe: East Africa's Swahili Coast
The Swahili people of the East African coast enjoyed a golden age from 1200 to 1500. They become part of an enormous Muslim trade network. Their city-states grew and competed. Because it controlled the gold trade, the city-state of Kilwa was the most prosperous and powerful until its collapse in the 16th century.

Library/Media Center Research Log   63

HOW TO USE THE STUDENT STUDY GUIDES TO
THE MEDIEVAL & EARLY MODERN WORLD

Each book in The Medieval & Early Modern World *introduces you to compelling adventures of fascinating men and women living at an amazing time. You will meet artists and warriors, rulers and scientists, merchants, traders, and slaves. You'll experience their lives close up, through diaries, letters, poems, songs, and myths.*

The events of the medieval and early modern time period changed the whole world forever. The foundations of international politics, the boundaries of countries and empires, the roots of educational and religious institutions—all were established during this rich, electrifying period. We can't fully understand our world today without understanding how it connects with these times.

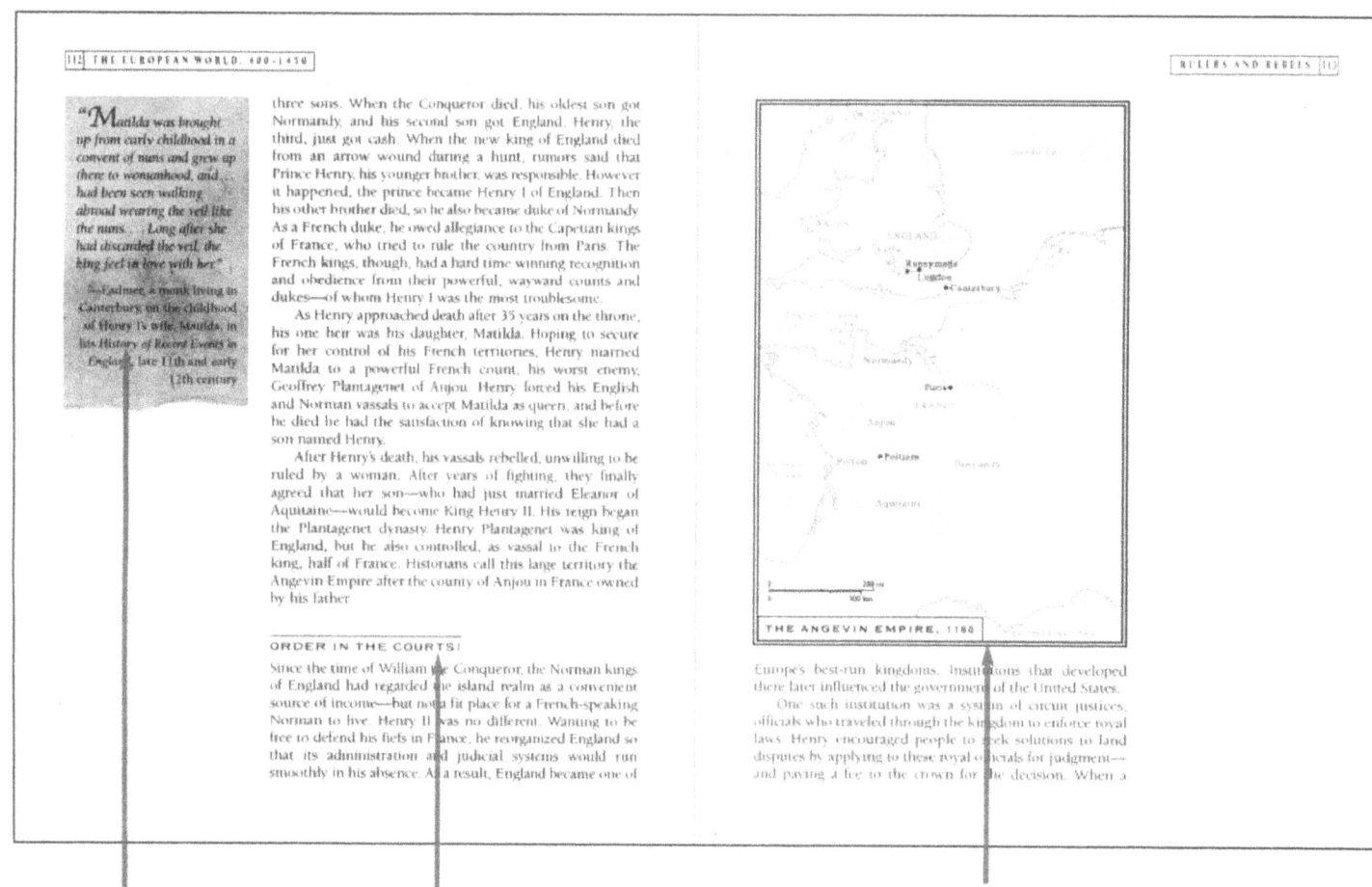

Short quotes in sidebars tell about life in the words of someone living at the time.

Subheads give clues to the content to follow.

Geography has a lot to do with history. Maps show the locations of important places and supply a geographic context for important events.

This study guide will help you as you read the books in the series. It will help you learn and enjoy history while building thinking and writing skills. And it will help you pass important tests. The sample pages below show the books' special features. But before you begin reading the book or using this guide, be sure to have a notebook or extra paper and a pen handy to make a history journal. A dictionary and thesaurus will help you too. A special tip: Before you start a new chapter, read the two-part chapter title and predict what you will learn from the chapter. Check to see if you were right at the end.

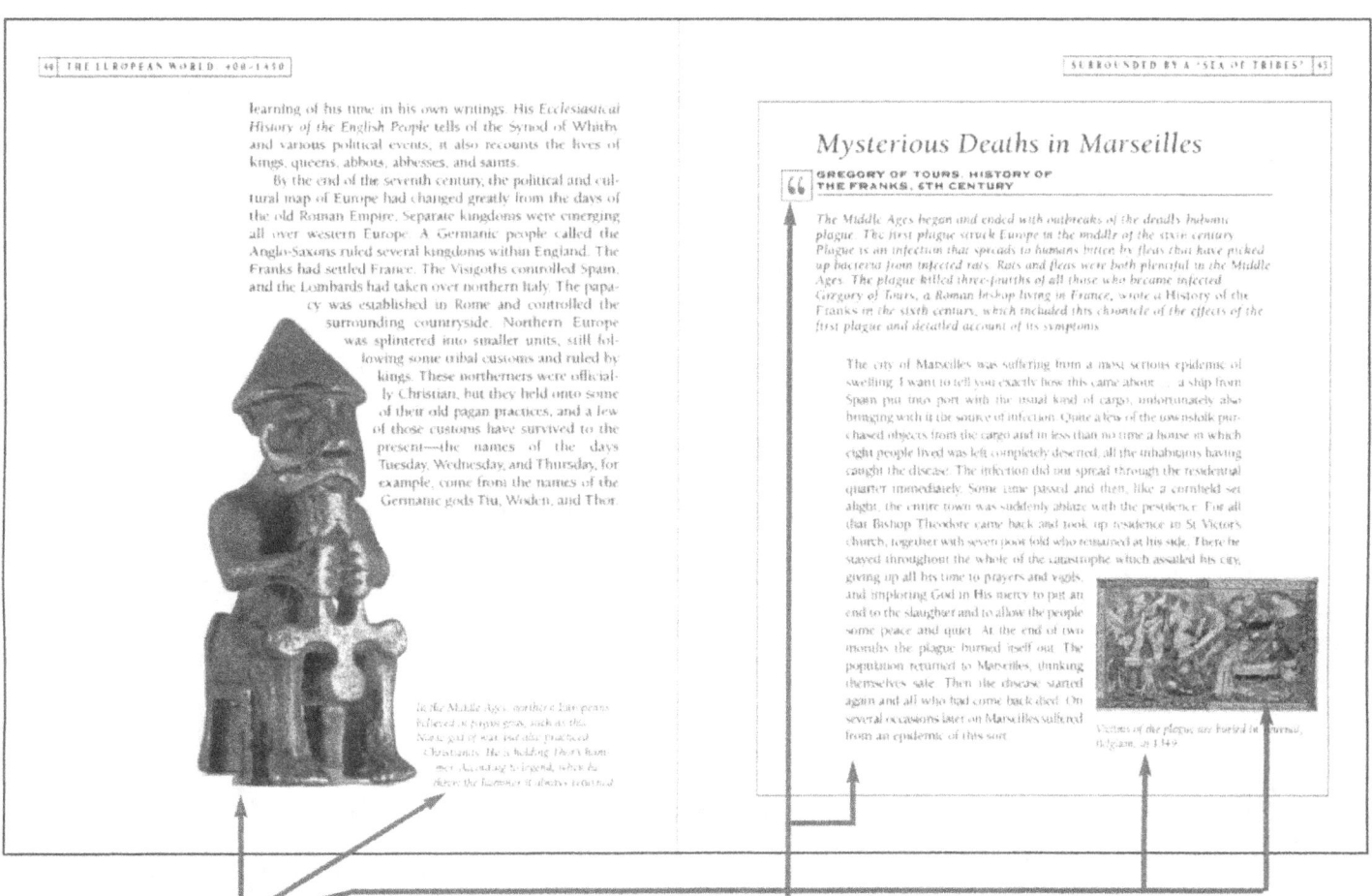

Pictures, often of artifacts, show distinctive art and design of the times. Read the captions to learn even more than is in the text.

Every chapter has a long primary source quote that takes you back in time to the scene of a significant action in a dramatic, powerful, first-person way. Look for these longer quotations marked by quotation marks followed by the source of the work.

On the next pages you will find models of graphic organizers. You will need these to do the activities for each chapter on the pages after that. Go back to the book as often as you need to.

GRAPHIC ORGANIZERS

As you read and study history, geography, and the social sciences, you'll start to collect a lot of information. Using a graphic organizer is one way to make information clearer and easier to understand. You can choose from different types of organizers, depending on the information.

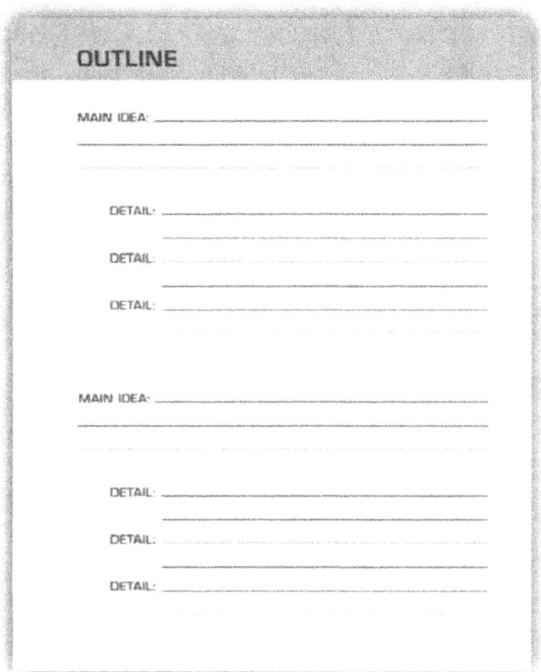

Outline
To build an outline, first identify your main idea. Write this at the top. Then, in the lines below, list the details that support the main idea. Keep adding main ideas and details as you need to.

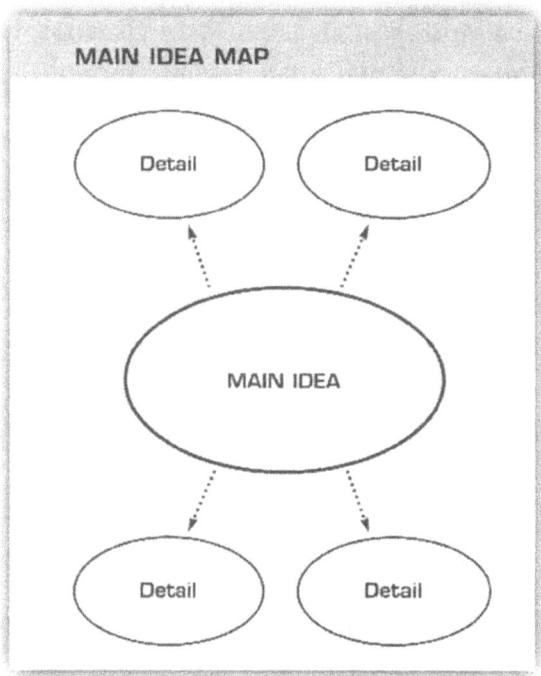

Main Idea Map
Write down your main idea in the central circle. Write details in the connecting circles.

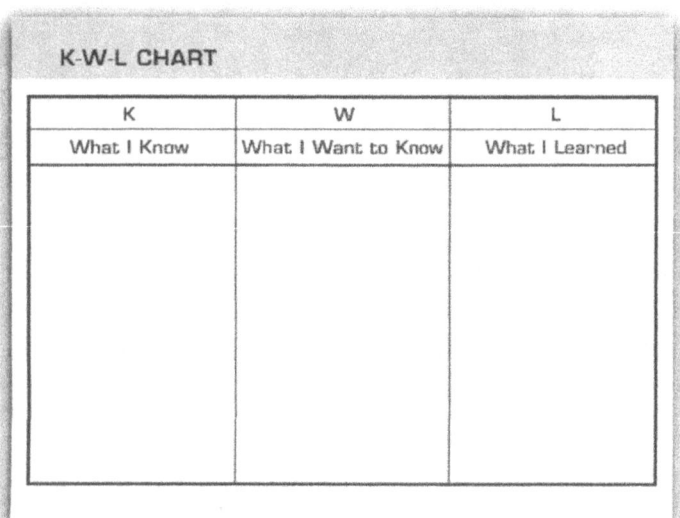

K-W-L Chart
Before you read a chapter, write down what you already know about a subject in the left column. Then write what you want to know in the center column. Then write what you learned in the last column. You can make a two-column version of this. Write what you know in the left and what you learned after reading the chapter.

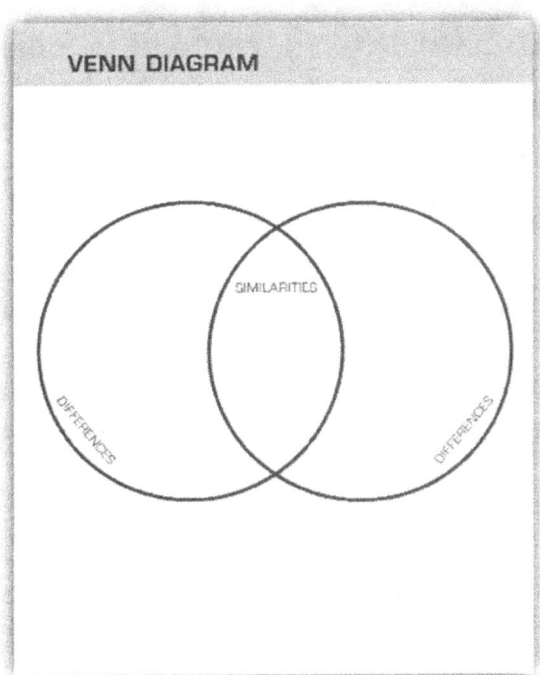

Venn Diagram
These overlapping circles show differences and similarities among topics. Each topic is shown as a circle. Any details the topics have in common go in the areas where those circles overlap. List the differences where the circles do not overlap.

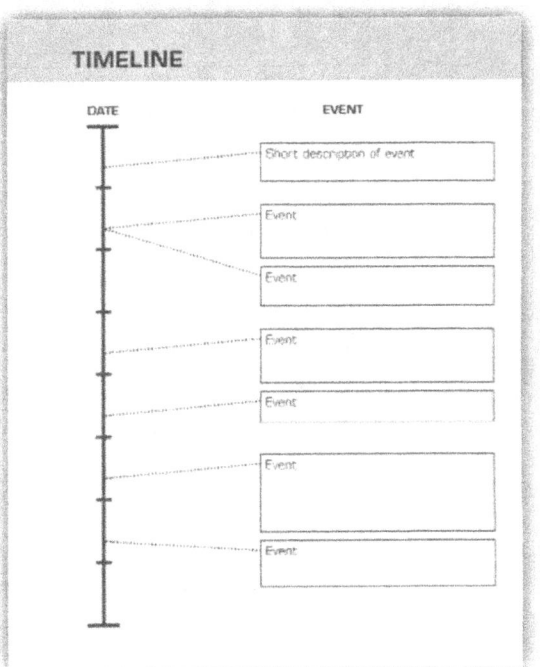

Timeline
A timeline divides a time period into equal chunks of time. Then it shows when events happened during that time. Decide how to divide up the timeline. Then write events in the boxes to the right when they happened. Connect them to the date line.

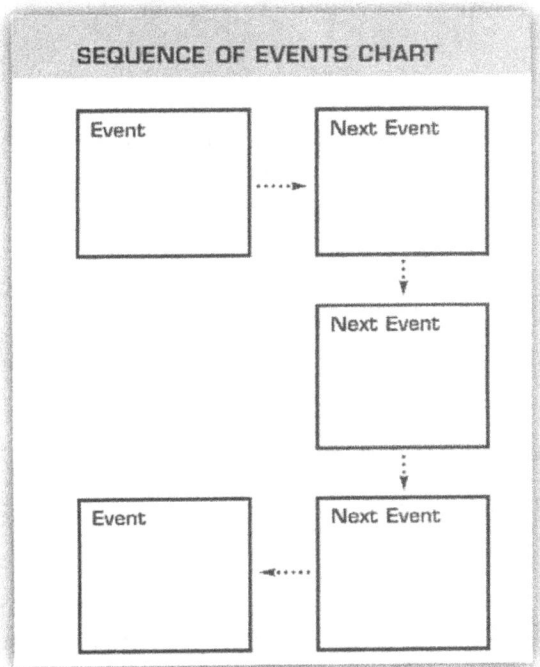

Sequence of Events Chart
Historical events bring about changes. These result in other events and changes. A sequence of events chart uses linked boxes to show how one event leads to another, and then another.

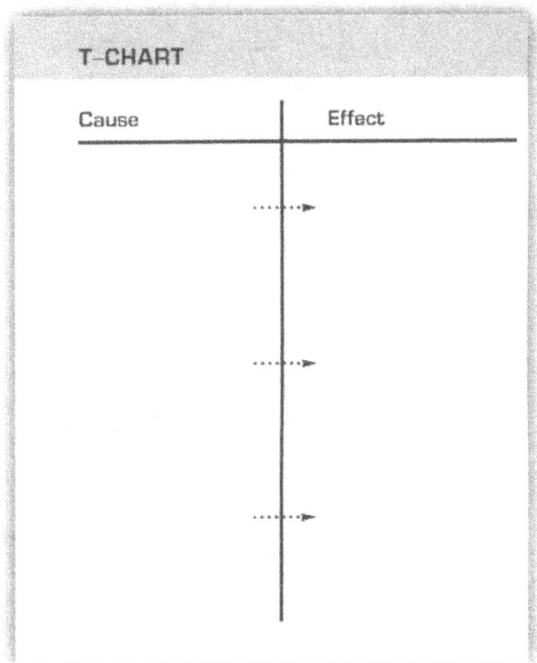

T-Chart
Use this chart to separate information into two columns. To separate causes and effects, list events, or causes, in one column. In the other column, list the change, or effect, each event brought about.

REPORTS AND SPECIAL PROJECTS

There's always more to find out about the African and Middle Eastern World during the Middle Ages. Take a look at the Further Reading section at the end of the book (pages 166–168). Here you'll find a number of books on different topics relating to medieval history. Many of them will be available in your school or local public library.

GETTING STARTED

Explore the Further Reading section for any of these reasons.

— You're curious and want to learn more about a particular topic.

— You want to do a research report on Africa and Middle East.

— You still have questions about something covered in the book.

— You need more information for a special classroom project.

What's the best way to find the books that will help you the most?

LOOK AT THE SUBHEADS

The books are organized by topic. The subhead "Forest Kingdoms" tells you where to find books about the civilizations of West Africa such as Nigeria and Benin. Go to "Ottoman Empire" to learn more about the rise and fall of the Turks. Other subheads include "North Africa and Spain," "Sudanic Kingdoms," and "The Swahili." Let the subheads give you ideas for reports and special projects.

LOOK AT THE BOOK TITLES

The titles of the books can tell you a lot about what's inside. The books listed under "Arts and Sciences" will give you several suggestions for learning more about Islamic architecture and literature, for example.

LOOK FOR GENERAL REFERENCES

This section also lists general books, which are useful starting points for further research. "General Works" will list titles that provide a broad overview of history in Africa and the Middle East in medieval times. Judge by the titles which books will be the most useful to you. Other references include:

— Dictionaries

— Encyclopedias

— Atlases

OTHER RESOURCES

Information comes in all kinds of formats. Use the book to learn about primary sources. Go to the library for videos, DVDs, and audio materials. And don't forget about the Internet!

AUDIO-VISUAL MATERIALS

Your school or local library can offer documentary videos and DVDs on early humankind, as well as audio materials. If you have access to a computer, explore the sites listed on the section titled Websites (page 169) for some good jumping-off points. These are organized by topic, with brief descriptions of what you'll find on the site. Many websites list additional reading, as well as other Internet links you can visit.

What you've learned about medieval Africa and the Middle East so far is just a beginning. Learning more is an ongoing adventure!

CHAPTER 1
CAMELS, CARAVANS, AND THE KA'BA: THE ARABIAN PENINSULA AROUND 600

CHAPTER SUMMARY
Traders from the east and west made long, dangerous trips across the desert to exchange goods in Mecca.

ACCESS
What do you think it would have been like to live in the desert 1,400 years ago? Chapter 1 describes life along the trading routes of Arabia in the 6th century. To organize information about the different groups of people in the chapter, make a 4-column chart in your history journal. Label the columns: *caravan guide*, *Bedouin*, *Quraysh tribe*, and *other religious groups*. Then write the information you learn about each group as you read the chapter.

WORD BANK
caravan   shaykh (shake)   Ka'ba (KAH-bah)   trade   Bedouin (BEH-doo-in)   nomads

Choose words from the Word Bank to complete the sentences. One word is not used at all.

1. The _____ guide and his camels traveled for many days across the desert.

2. Statues were housed inside the _____.

3. A caravan guide would _____ spices and perfumes.

4. The _____ people attacked the caravans.

5. The _____ moved from place to place.

WORD PLAY
Look up the word that you did not use in the dictionary. Write a sentence using that word.

_____

WITH A PARENT OR PARTNER
The Ka'ba is a holy building for a particular religion. Many faiths have holy buildings. How many other kinds of holy buildings can you think of? Make a list and ask a parent or partner to make a list, too. Combine your lists to see how many different examples of holy buildings you thought of.

CRITICAL THINKING
CAUSE AND EFFECT

The reason that something happens is called a *cause*. The thing that happens is known as the *effect*. Writers often use signal words such as *because*, *so*, or *as a result* to signal a cause-and-effect relationship. Look at this example.

CAUSE	EFFECT
The houses in the desert are made of brick and stone with a flat top,	SO the hot rays of the sun are deflected.

Think about the conditions in the desert described in Chapter 1 and how these conditions affected daily life for the people who lived there. Match the "causes" in the left column with the "effects" in the right column. (There is one extra effect.)

CAUSE	EFFECT
1. People usually wear loose, white cotton gowns,	a. SO there are many wars over the areas where there is water.
2. Sacred statues and stones are housed at the Ka'ba,	b. SO they are used to transport goods through the hot, dry desert.
3. Camels are strong animals that can go a long time without water,	c. SO tribal elders can reject the shaykh's decisions.
4. Water is difficult to find in the desert,	d. SO people go to worship there.
5. There is no one who is completely in power in the desert,	e. SO people felt safe to come to Mecca during Ramadan.
6. The Bedouin agreed not to attack for one month each year,	f. SO the Bedouin are free to attack caravan groups.
	g. SO their clothing won't stick and the heat of the sun will reflect away.

WITH A PARENT OR PARTNER

When you complete the exercise, work with a parent or partner to read each cause-and-effect pairing aloud. Talk about any matches that may not be correct. For an added challenge, try to think of a cause that would go with the extra effect, using information from the chapter. Write cause and effect on the lines below.

_____

_____

WORKING WITH PRIMARY SOURCES

Khansa was a poet who lived near Mecca and Medina in the late 6th century. Many of her poems are about her two brothers, who were killed in fights with neighboring tribes in Arabia. Read the following excerpt written in honor of Khansa's brother Sakhr.

> Many was the guest who arrived by night or the man who was
> Seeking protection, [people] whose hearts were alarmed at
> Every sound.
> He treated [such people] kindly and made them safe, so that
> Their state was free from every pressing need.
> Ah, O Sakhr, I shall [never] forget you until I part from my
> Soul and my grave is cut.
> The rising of the sun reminds of Sakhr, and I remember
> Him every time the sun sets.

1. According to the poem, how did Sahkr help people?

2. What is the poet's mood?

3. What does the poet mean by, "Ah, O Sakhr, I shall [never] forget you until I part from my Soul and my grave is cut"?

4. How does Khansa express that she will always remember her brother?

WRITE ABOUT IT

In your history journal, write a diary entry as if you were a Bedouin in 6th-century Arabia. Describe what your life is like and the events of the day as well as your response to the conflicts that your tribe may face. Be sure to use descriptive words that tell how things look, sound, feel, or taste. Consider using such words as *hot*, *dangerous*, or *tiring*.

HISTORY JOURNAL

Don't forget to share your history journal with your classmates, and ask if you can see what their journals look like. You might be surprised—and get some new ideas.

THE AFRICAN & MIDDLE EASTERN WORLD, 600–1500

ALL OVER THE MAP
INTERACTION

Study the map below. Then do the following exercises and answer the questions in your history journal.

1. On the map, draw a route the caravan guide described in the chapter would have followed. The guide would have started in Mecca, and then made two journeys: one to Egypt and one to Persia.

2. Write the names of the goods the caravan guide traded in the various places. For example, at Yemen, he might have traded for incense and perfumes.

3. Use the mileage scale to calculate the distance of the trade route from the beginning of the caravan's journey to Egypt and then to Persia. Write the distances here.

_____

_____

4. What factors made traveling in the desert dangerous?

5. Explain why caravans took the risks of desert travel to trade goods between faraway cities.

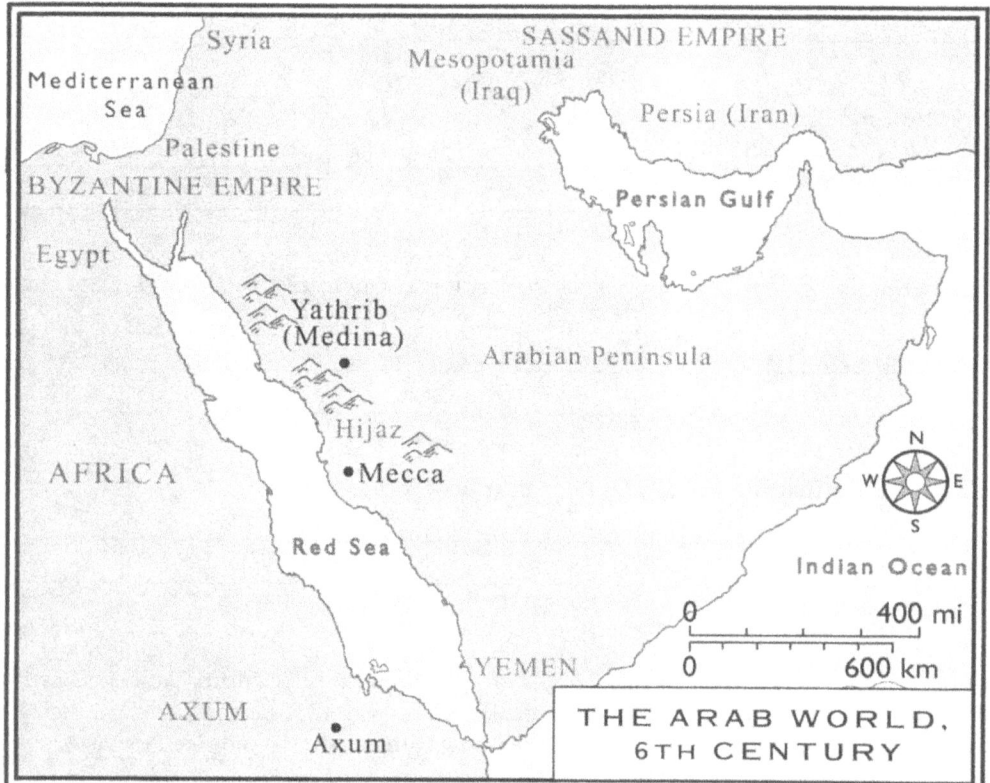

14   CHAPTER 1

CHAPTER 2
THE MESSENGER OF ALLAH: MUHAMMAD AND THE BEGINNING OF ISLAM

CHAPTER SUMMARY
The prophet Muhammad brought many polytheistic people of Arabia together under the belief in one God. This monotheistic religion was called Islam.

ACCESS
To organize the information in this chapter, take notes in your history journal about the important events in Muhammad's life. Number the events in order as you write about them and put them into a sequence of events chart (see the graphic organizer on page 9 of this study guide).

CAST OF CHARACTERS
Write a few sentences to explain why each person was important.

Muhammad _____

_____

_____

_____

Abu Talib _____

_____

_____

_____

Khadija _____

_____

_____

_____

WORD BANK
revelation   meditation   persecution   pilgrimage   convert   prophet

Choose words from the Word Bank to complete the sentences. One word is not used at all.

1. Muhammad's accounts of his visions helped _____ new followers to Islam.

2. While Muhammad was in prayer and _____, he had a _____.

3. The faithful followers of the _____ Muhammad made a _____ to Mecca.

WORD PLAY
Look up the word you did not use in the dictionary. Write a sentence using that word.

_____

THE AFRICAN & MIDDLE EASTERN WORLD, 600–1500

WITH A PARENT OR PARTNER

Identify which words below are nouns, and which are verbs by circling "noun" or "verb." With a parent or partner, figure out how you could change the nouns into verbs, or vice versa. Experiment by going back to the root word, and by adding or subtracting suffixes and letters. Then write your variation on the line, and identify whether it is a noun or a verb. See the first example. (Note that one word can be both a noun and a verb in its current form.)

1. Persecute   (verb)   (~~noun~~) variation: persecution (noun)
2. Meditation (verb)   (noun) variation:_____
3. Convert   (verb)   (noun) variation:_____
4. Revelation (verb)   (noun) variation:_____

CRITICAL THINKING
MAIN IDEA AND SUPPORTING DETAILS

Use the outline below to organize main ideas and details from the chapter. In the lines below each main idea, write details that support that main idea.

1. **MAIN IDEA:** Muhammad was an important figure in the history of islam.

   DETAIL: _____

   DETAIL: _____

   DETAIL: _____

2. **MAIN IDEA:** Muhammad was a strong leader.

   DETAIL: _____

   DETAIL: _____

   DETAIL: _____

3. **MAIN IDEA:** Muhammad and his followers fought against people who refused to live peacefully with them.

   DETAIL: _____

   DETAIL: _____

   DETAIL: _____

4. **MAIN IDEA:** Muhammad established a new way of life for his followers.

   DETAIL: _____

   DETAIL: _____

   DETAIL: _____

WORKING WITH PRIMARY SOURCES

This excerpt from the Quran describes the rewards that will be offered to Muslims who do good works and believe in God.

> God has prepared a great reward and they have nothing to fear. [They] shall be served with silver dishes, and . . . cups brim-full with ginger-flavored water, [and rewarded] with robes of silk and the delights of Paradise. Reclining there upon soft couches, they shall feel neither the scorching heat nor the biting cold. Trees will spread their shade around them, and fruits will hang in clusters over them.

WRITE ABOUT IT

Write a short essay about this passage, discussing the importance of the rewards. Include a list of all the rewards mentioned in the passage, and an explanation of what makes them rewards. Explain why the rewards would be particularly appealing to Muslims living in a desert environment.

_____
_____
_____
_____
_____
_____

Read the following excerpts from the Quran about the importance of being generous. Then answer the following questions.

> Righteous is the one who believes in God and the last day, the angels and Scripture and the prophets; gives wealth, however cherished, to relatives and orphans, the needy and travelers and beggars, and for freeing slaves; and prays and gives [donations or alms].

Muhammad preached a very similar message to his followers:

> Did [God] not find you an orphan and give you shelter? Did he not find you destitute and enrich you? So then, do no wrong to the orphan, [nor] the suppliant do not turn away and make the grace of your Lord your constant theme.

1. What main theme do both passages have in common?

_____
_____
_____

2. Based on these passages, what should one do to be a good Muslim?

_____
_____
_____

3. Look up any words you don't know in the dictionary for their definitions. Then look them up in a thesaurus and write them down here.

_____
_____
_____

ALL OVER THE MAP

Study the map of the Arabian Peninsula below. Then do the following exercises.

1. Each of these years marks a date that a battle took place on the Arabian Peninsula. Write each date on the map at the location where the battle occurred. Then on the lines below, give a brief description of each battle (why did the battle start; who fought whom; what was the outcome) next to each date.

   500 _____

   570 _____

   624 _____

   625 _____

   627 _____

2. Write a paragraph that summarizes this period of fighting: Why did fighting take place, and what were the consequences of the battles?

   _____

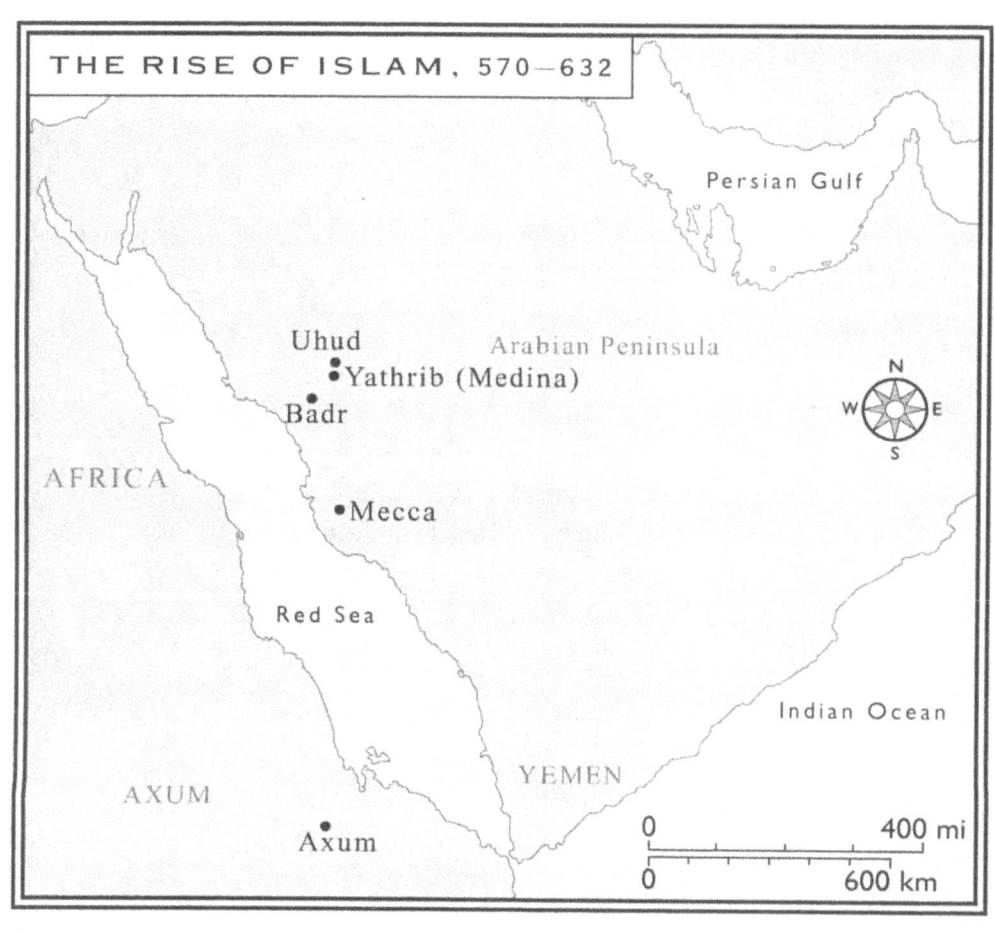

CHAPTER 2

CHAPTER 3
THE SWORD OF ALLAH: THE ISLAMIC EXPANSION

CHAPTER SUMMARY
The Islamic leaders after Muhammad helped to spread Islamic rule beyond the Arabian Peninsula, across northern Africa and into Spain.

ACCESS
How are the leaders in the United States, such as the president, chosen? How is this different from the way royal leaders, such as the queen of England, are selected? In your history journal, make a two-column chart. It the first column, write the name of a person who is a leader. In the second column, write how that person became a leader. Add as many people you can think of from the present time, or historical figures. As you read, add the names and information about the Islamic leaders discussed in the chapter.

CAST OF CHARACTERS
Write a few sentences about why the following people were important.

Abu Bakr _____
_____
_____
_____

Umar _____
_____
_____
_____

Tariq (tar EEK) _____
_____
_____
_____

WORD BANK
heir   resisters   alliance   deputy

Choose words from the Word Bank to complete the sentences. One word is not used.

1. Many Muslims thought that Ali was Muhammad's rightful _____.
2. Later leaders of the Muslim faith called themselves *caliph*, which means _____.
3. The Muslims fought against the Byzantines and met with pockets of _____.

WORD PLAY

Look up the word that you did not use in the dictionary. Write a sentence using that word.

WITH A PARENT OR PARTNER

The word *resister* means "one who resists." The suffix *–er* when added to a verb refers to the person or thing that performs the action of the verb. (In this example, the verb is "to resist.") With a parent or partner, make a list in your journal of as many words as you can think of that end in *–er* that also refer to a person or thing that performs an action.

CRITICAL THINKING
SEQUENCE OF EVENTS

The sentences below list events in the expansion of Islam. In the sequence of events diagram provided, write the numbers of the events in the correct order to show how Islam grew and spread.

1. Islam spread throughout the Arabian Peninsula.
2. Umar became the new Muslim leader.
3. The prophet Muhammad died suddenly.
4. Tariq and his men took much of the Spanish peninsula for Islam.
5. Abu Bakr was named the new Muslim leader.

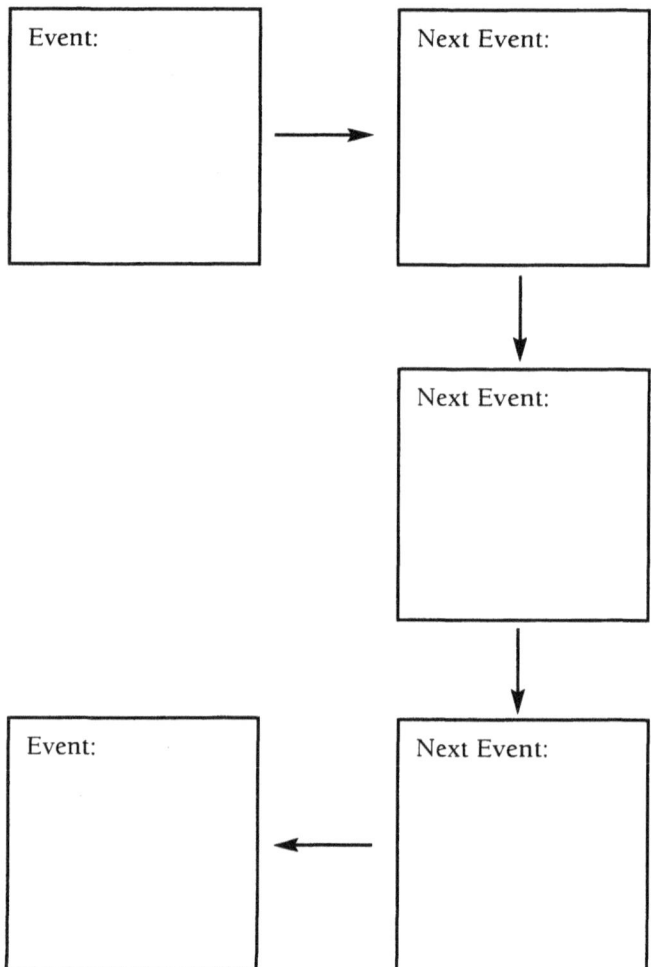

WORKING WITH PRIMARY SOURCES

Read the following excerpts about the Berber people. Then answer the questions that follow.

From *Muqaddimah* by Tunisian historian Ibn Khaldun (1377):

> [The Berbers] belong to a powerful, formidable, brave and numerous people; a true people like so many others the world has seen—like the Arabs, the Persians, the Greeks and the Romans.

From Strabo, a Roman geographer writing in the 1st century BCE:

> [The Berbers] wander from place to place with their flocks. . . . Their flocks and herds are small in size, whether sheep, goats, or oxen; the dogs also, though fierce and quarrelsome, are small. . . . They have no oil, but use butter and fat instead. . . . They live also upon the flesh and blood of animals, milk, and cheese.

1. List all the adjectives used in both passages that describe the Berbers.

2. Which excerpt gives you more facts about the Berber way of life?

3. What do you think is the main point of each excerpt? Explain your answer using examples from the quotations.

4. What is Ibn Khaldun's opinion of the Berbers? Explain your answer.

5. Write a paragraph comparing the two quotations. Consider which source is more objective, and which is more descriptive about the Berbers. What does each quotation say about the writer?

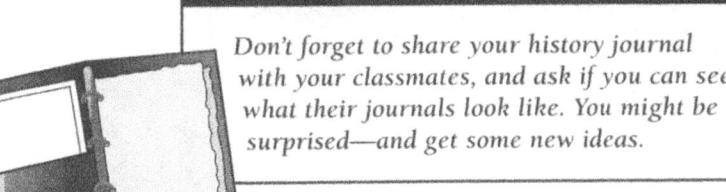

HISTORY JOURNAL

Don't forget to share your history journal with your classmates, and ask if you can see what their journals look like. You might be surprised—and get some new ideas.

THE AFRICAN & MIDDLE EASTERN WORLD, 600–1500

ALL OVER THE MAP
REGION

The map below shows the expansion of Islam. Using the information in the chapter, indicate on the map when each area was acquired during the Islamic expansion. Use a different shading pattern or color for each of the areas, and write the correct dates from this list:

632–634   634–651   665–680   711–716

Then shade the boxes in the legend and add the dates to explain the map.

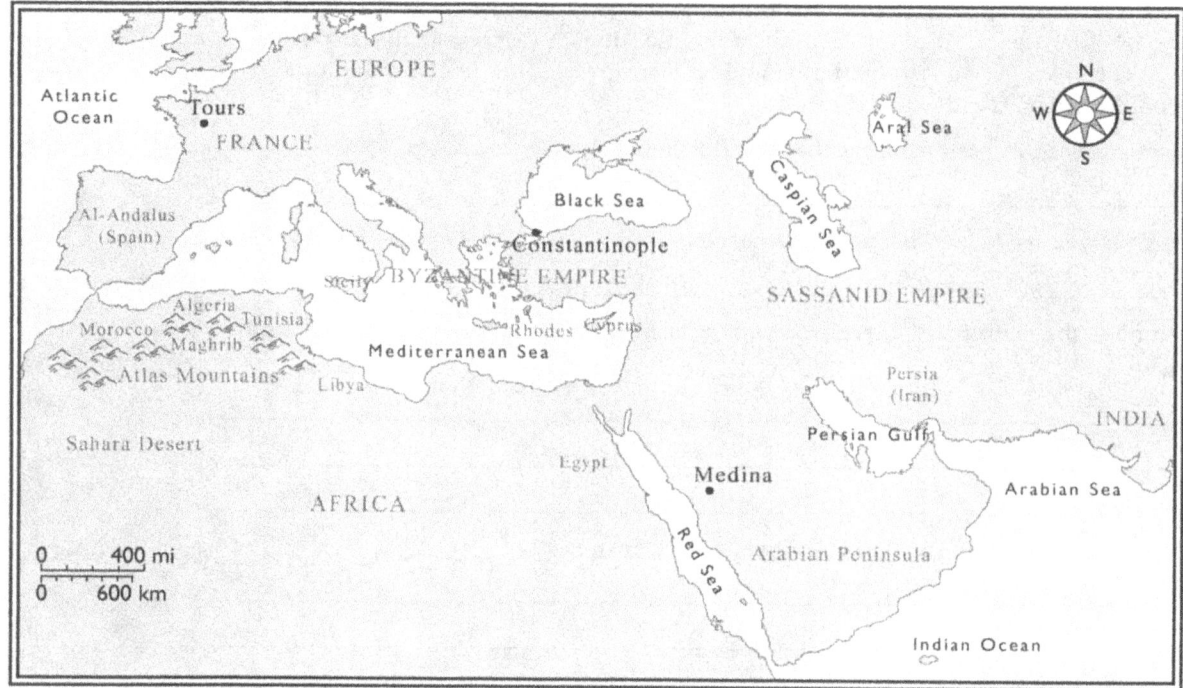

The Expansion of Islam

| | Arabian Peninsula ____-____ | | Sassanid Empire ____-____ |
| | Algeria and Morocco ____-____ | | Spain ____-____ |

22 CHAPTER 3

CHAPTER 4: MANAGING THE EMPIRE: ISLAM GROWS INTO AN EMPIRE OF FAITH

CHAPTER SUMMARY

Islamic leaders could not decide on a clear successor to Umar, and eventually factions developed within the Muslim communities.

ACCESS

In this chapter, various Islamic leaders were assassinated, or killed, by people who did not want them to be leaders. Think about other important leaders in history, including American presidents, who were assassinated. Why might someone have wanted to stop these leaders?

CAST OF CHARACTERS

Write a sentence to explain the importance of each person below.

Umar _____

_____

Uthman _____

_____

Ali _____

_____

Muawiyah _____

_____

WORD BANK

diplomacy   factions   administrator   *zakat*   *jizya*

Choose words from the Word Bank to complete the sentences. One word is not used at all.

1. A charitable tax paid by Muslims is called _____.
2. An _____ is someone who manages and supervises.
3. Muslims divided into _____ because different groups believed different things.
4. The Muslim leader dealt with other groups with _____.
5. A tax paid by non-Muslims is called a _____.

WITH A PARENT OR PARTNER

In your history journal, write the words *diplomacy*, *diplomat*, and *diplomatic*. Look up these words in the dictionary and write a few sentences to explain how these words are related. Consider the following questions: Which words are nouns, and which are adjectives? Which words describe a person? Also look up the words in a thesaurus and list other words that have similar meanings.

CRITICAL THINKING
COMPARE AND CONTRAST

The phrases below describe the Islamic leaders who came after Umar. The Venn diagram below has three circles, one for each of these leaders. Write the numbers of the phrases below in the correct circles. The numbers that apply to only one leader go in that person's circle. The numbers that describe two leaders go in the area where those two circles overlap. Numbers that describe all three leaders go in the area where all three circles overlap.

1. organized the messages of Muhammad
2. was assassinated
3. member of the Umayyad family
4. called "imam"
5. moved Muslim capital to Damascus
6. set up a treasury for the tax funds
7. fought with his troops at Siffin
8. was a caliph
9. supported by Shiite Muslims
10. recognized by Sunni Muslims as legitimate leader

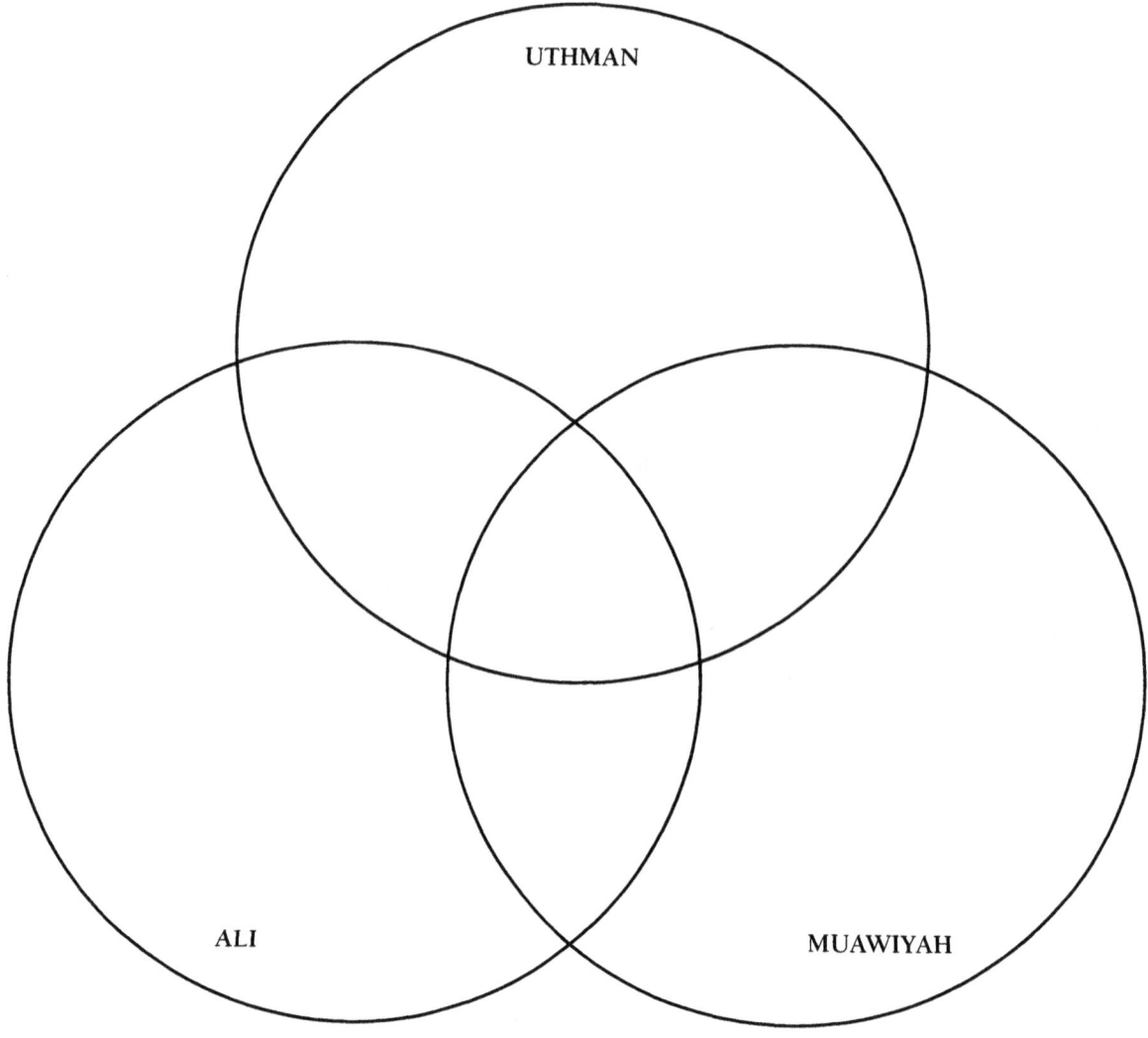

WORKING WITH PRIMARY SOURCES

The History of al-Tabari, Vol XVII: The First Civil War

The following excerpt describes a meeting among a group of Ali's supporters. Answer the questions that follow in complete sentences.

> [Some of the men] met together and . . . then said, "By God it is not fitting that a people . . . should prefer this world to the commanding of good . . . and the proclaiming of truth . . . so let us go out, brethren of ours, from this settlement [Ali's camp] whose people are wicked to one of the districts of the mountains or to one of the towns rejecting these innovations that lead [us] astray.

1. Why did the men decide that the rest of Ali's supporters were wicked?

2. What are they referring to when they say "this world"?

3. What do they mean by "the proclaiming of truth"?

4. "Brethren" is another word for "brothers," but we know that the men speaking were not actually related. What do they mean by using this word to describe one another?

5. In what ways is this statement like a pep rally, a speech meant to persuade people to take a certain action? In your answer, use examples of words and phrases meant to influence the audience.

COMPREHENSION

Read the paragraph on page 48 that begins "Uthman's cousin Muawiyah, the Syrian governor, accused Ali . . . " and the paragraph after that. Then answer the following questions.

1. To what did Ali agree?

2. According to al-Tabari, how did some of the men respond to Ali's decision?

3. What action did the men take after their meeting?

WRITE ABOUT IT

Imagine you are Ali, and a group of men told you they did not agree with your decision to have a discussion with Muawiyah's side. How would you convince these men of your decision? In your history journal, write what you would say to these people.

ALL OVER THE MAP

Study the map below. Then answer the questions.

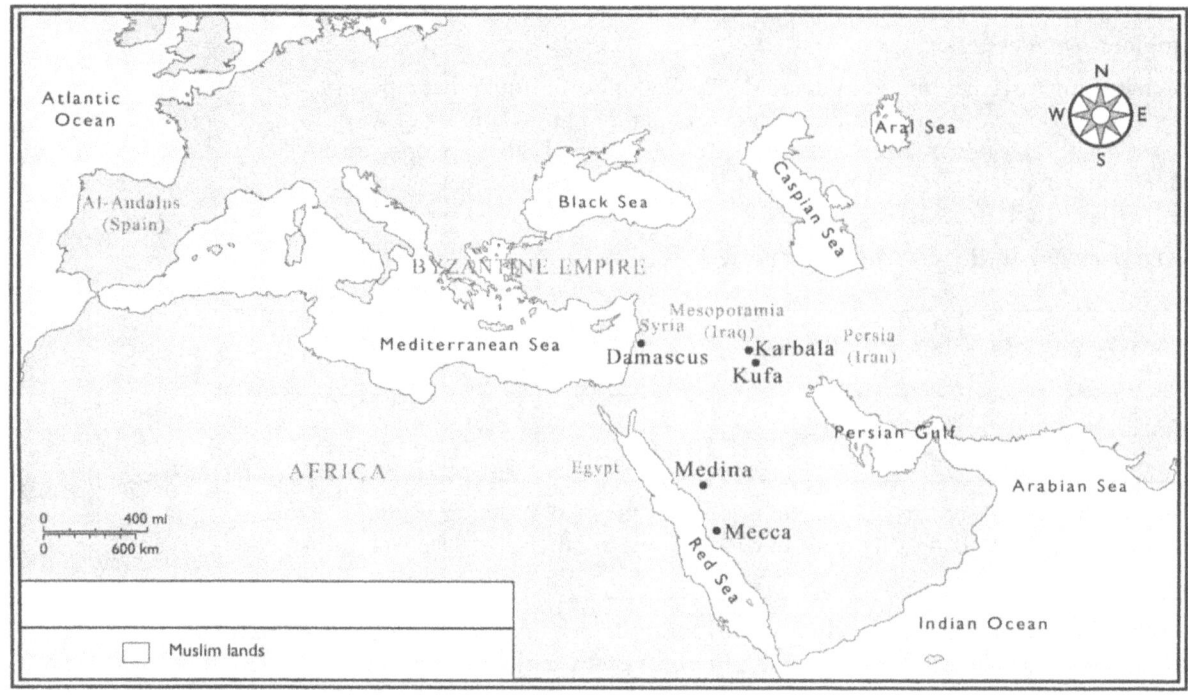

1. Use shading or a pattern to show the extent of Muslim lands by 749. Then key this pattern in the legend.

2. Draw the path Muawiyah may have followed in moving the capital from Medina to Damascus. Use the scale to measure the distance between Medina and Damascus. How many miles did Muawiyah travel? _____

3. List the bodies of water that border the Muslim Empire.

   _____
   _____
   _____
   _____

4. Why might these bodies of water be important to the Muslim Empire?

   _____
   _____
   _____

CHAPTER 4

CHAPTER 5
THE HOUSE OF ISLAM: THE FIRST WORLDWIDE CIVILIZATION

CHAPTER SUMMARY
During the Abbasid caliphate, the Muslim Empire grew rapidly and became an important center for trade.

ACCESS
Ibn Battuta was an explorer who traveled all over the Muslim world. He kept a journal about the important things he saw and the people he met. He also used details to describe what he saw. As you read the chapter, write the main ideas you find on the outline below. Add details that support the main ideas on the lines.

MAIN IDEA:

    DETAIL: _____

    DETAIL: _____

    DETAIL: _____

MAIN IDEA:

    DETAIL: _____

    DETAIL: _____

    DETAIL: _____

MAIN IDEA:

    DETAIL: _____

    DETAIL: _____

    DETAIL: _____

MAIN IDEA:

    DETAIL: _____

    DETAIL: _____

    DETAIL: _____

CAST OF CHARACTERS
Write one sentence each to explain the importance of the following people.

Ibn Battuta _____

Abu Jafar al-Mansur _____

Fatima _____

WHAT HAPPENED WHEN?

State what happened on each of the dates below.

662 _____

749–750 _____

874 _____

969 _____

1258 _____

WORD BANK

descendants geographic radiating provinces lavish ornate

Choose words from the Word Bank to complete the sentences. One word is not used at all.

1. Muhammad's clan and _____ continued to receive support payments.
2. Each of the _____ of the empire was run by a governor.
3. Baghdad was at the _____ center of the empire.
4. The caliphs lived in a very _____ way.
5. As the city grew, it seemed to be _____ from the center.

WORD PLAY

Look up in a dictionary the word that you did not use. Write a sentence using that word.

_____

WITH A PARENT OR PARTNER

In your history journal, list all the English words you can think of that begin with the prefix *geo-*. Ask a parent or partner to make a list, too. Compare your lists. Can you figure out what the prefix *geo-* means? Make a guess before going to a dictionary.

CRITICAL THINKING
FACT OR OPINION?

A fact is a statement that can be proved. An opinion judges things or people, but it cannot be proved or disproved. Label each sentence from the chapter "F" if it is a fact, or "O" if it is an opinion.

_____ 1. The Persian mawalis were being treated like second-class citizens.

_____ 2. The best spot for the new capital was in Baghdad.

_____ 3. Al-Tabari spent too much money on the new palace.

_____ 4. The caliphs divided the empire into many provinces.

_____ 5. Muslims controlled the major Indian Ocean sea lanes.

_____ 6. The Abbasid caliphs lived far too lavishly.

_____ 7. The caliphs desire for luxury goods helped industries to grow.

_____ 8. Syrians treated their domestic slaves well.

_____ 9. The Shiites called their rightful leaders "imam."

_____ 10. The Seljuk sultans took political power from the caliphs.

WORKING WITH PRIMARY SOURCES

Geographical Dictionary by Yaqut bin Abdallah Al-Hamawi (13th century)

Read the following description of Baghdad, written by a Greek slave who was later released. He describes the city as it was in its "glory days," in the 10th century. Then answer the following questions.

> The city of Baghdad formed two vast semi-circles on the right and left banks of the Tigris, twelve miles in diameter. The numerous suburbs, covered with parks, gardens, villas and beautiful promenades, and plentifully supplied with rich bazaars, and finely built mosques and baths, stretched for a considerable distance on both sides of the river. . . . The palace of the Caliph stood in the midst of a vast park several hours in circumference which beside a menagerie and aviary comprised an enclosure for wild animals reserved for the chase. The palace grounds were laid out with gardens, and adorned with exquisite taste with plants, flowers, and trees, reservoirs and fountains, surrounded by sculptured figures. On this side of the river stood the palaces of the great nobles. . . .
>
> Baghdad was a veritable City of Palaces, not made of stucco and mortar, but of marble. . . . Both sides of the river were for miles fronted by the palaces, kiosks, gardens and parks of the grandees and nobles, marble steps led down to the water's edge, and the scene on the river was animated by thousands of gondolas, decked with little flags, dancing like sunbeams on the water, and carrying the pleasure-seeking Baghdad citizens from one part of the city to the other.

DRAWING CONCLUSIONS

1. What conclusions can you draw about Baghdad based on this description?

   _____
   _____
   _____

2. Circle the words or phrases that support the statement "Baghdad was a veritable City of Palaces."

3. What characteristics of Baghdad, described here, would have made it a particularly impressive place to visit back in the 10th century?

   _____
   _____
   _____

4. In your history journal, draw a map or town plan of the city, based on this description.

WRITE ABOUT IT

Think about where you live. How is your town or city divided into neighborhoods or sections? Choose a few neighborhoods of your town or city and write a paragraph about them in your history journal. How would you describe them to someone who's never been there? Describe the buildings, parks, stores, and other features.

GROUP TOGETHER

Wouldn't it be interesting to compare neighborhoods with other students? Get a few friends together and ask your teacher to help you organize a discussion group at school. Have one person take notes and another person present the group's ideas to class.

THE AFRICAN & MIDDLE EASTERN WORLD, 600–1500

ALL OVER THE MAP
MEASUREMENT

The map below shows important locations in the Abbasid Empire in 763. Complete the following exercises.

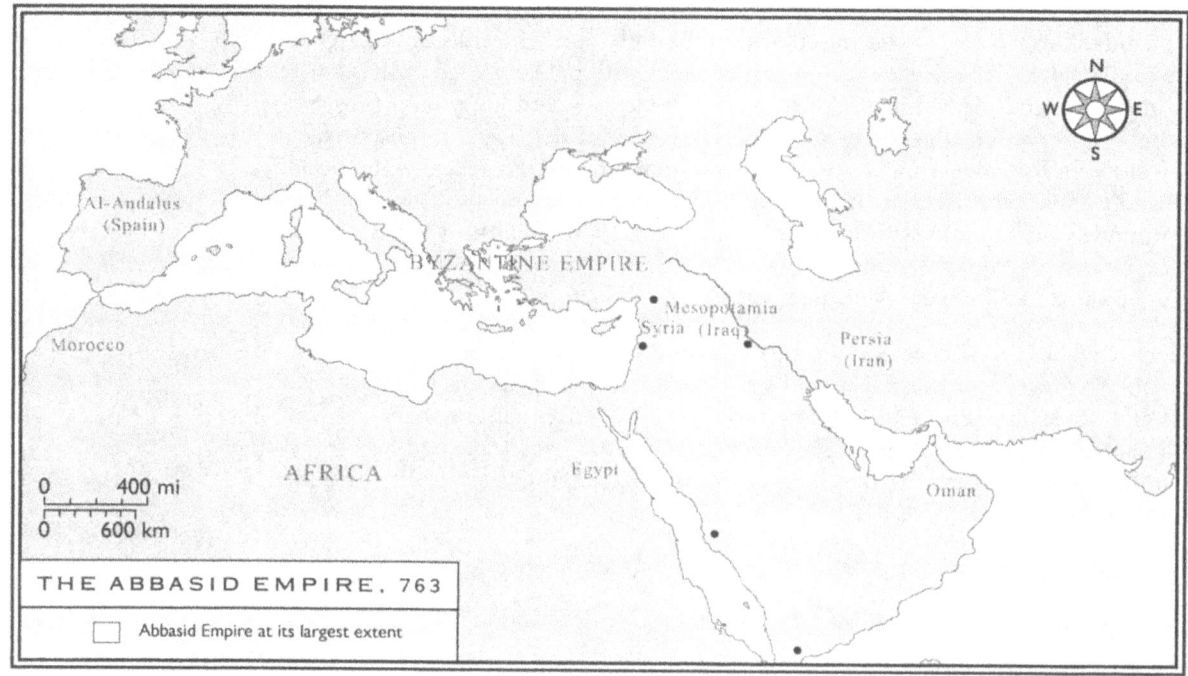

1. Use shading or a pattern to show the extent of the Abbasid Empire in 763. Key this pattern to the legend.
2. Label the major bodies of water that border the Abbasid Empire.
3. Locate and label Baghdad, the Abbasid capital, on the map.
4. Abu Jafar al-Mansur chose Baghdad as the capital because it was "near the geographic center of the empire." What aspects of the city's location make this true?

_____

_____

5. Locate and label the following cities:

   Aden

   Mecca

   Damascus

   Aleppo

6. Trace Ibn Battuta's pilgrimage from Morocco to Mecca.
7. What was Ibn Battuta's most likely route, by land or by water? Explain your answer.

_____

_____

8. Use the mileage scale to calculate the distance of this journey, and write it here.

_____

9. How far would pilgrims have to travel to Mecca from

   a) Aleppo? _____

   b) Aden? _____

   c) Damascus? _____

   d) Spain? _____

30 CHAPTER 5

CHAPTER 6
LIVING BY THE RULES: ULAMA AND PHILOSOPHERS

CHAPTER SUMMARY
Early Muslims developed ways of interpreting the Quran and teachings of Muhammad to determine how they were supposed to live.

ACCESS
People's actions during certain events can affect other people's lives or cause different events to happen. In the space below, create a two-column chart with the column headings *Cause* and *Effect*. As you read the chapter, think about the events and the actions of the people mentioned. In each column write whether you think this event or action is a cause or an effect. Complete each column so that every cause has an effect written next to it. Draw arrows from each cause to the matching effect.

Cause	Effect

CAST OF CHARACTERS
Write a complete sentence explaining why each character was important.

al-Ma'mun _____

Ahmad ibn Hanbal _____

Abu Hamid Muhammad al-Ghazali _____

WORD BANK

piety   hadiths   Sufis   *ulama*   Mutazilites   *tariqas*

Choose words from the Word Bank to complete the sentences. One word is not used at all.

1. Muhammad lived a life of _____ and was an example to others.
2. _____ were religious experts who served as judges in Islamic courts.
3. Sufis gradually organized themselves into associations, called _____.
4. Muslims repeated _____ as ways of remembering how Muhammad lived.
5. _____ believed that God gave humans free will to choose their own behavior.

WORD PLAY

Look up in a dictionary the word that you did not use. Write that word in a sentence. Write down any other interesting facts you can find about this word.

_____
_____
_____
_____

WITH A PARENT OR PARTNER

In your history journal, write the names of as many people you can think of who have lived lives of piety. Think of leaders and famous people, as well as people you know. Ask a parent or partner to make a list, too. Together discuss what these people did in their lives and how they behaved to show their piety.

CRITICAL THINKING
DRAWING CONCLUSIONS

Each of the sentences below in *italics* is taken from the chapter. Place a check mark in front of the conclusions that can be drawn from reading the sentence.

1. *The Quran stresses moral principles and guidelines about piety and justice. It provides only a few detailed instructions about ordinary living.*
    a) Early Muslims needed to find other ways to help them know how to live.
    b) Everyone was able to agree on how good Muslims should live and what they should believe.
    c) Non-Muslims weren't allowed to read the Quran.
    d) Muhammad was not interested in how Muslims lived from day to day.

2. *The religious scholars were not the only thinkers that the Abbasids encouraged.*
    a) But they did believe that the religious scholars were the most important.
    b) The Abbasids did not believe in the free exchange of ideas.
    c) This caused the religious scholars to change their ideas.
    d) They also supported other scholars and thinkers.

3. *In the end, Sufis even helped to expand the Islamic world beyond Arabian and Persian borders into Africa and Southeast Asia.*
    a) The Sufis wanted to spread Islam all over the world.
    b) The Sufis were very important to the Muslim religion.
    c) The Sufis needed to form organizations to keep control of Islam.
    d) Other parts of the world were hostile to Islam.

WORKING WITH PRIMARY SOURCES

Read the excerpt below of Ibn Battuta's observations about the Sufis. Then answer the questions that follow.

> ... after the mid-afternoon prayer drums and kettledrums were beaten .... After this they prayed the sunset prayer and brought in the meal consisting of rice-bread, fish, milk, and dates. After the night prayer they began to recite their litany.

1. Circle the words or phrases that tell the activities the Sufis participated in when they were not praying.

2. Summarize the daily routine of the Sufis.
   _____
   _____

3. At which times of day did the Sufis pray?
   _____

4. What conclusions can you draw about the Sufis, based on this description?
   _____
   _____

IDENTIFYING POINT OF VIEW

Ibn Battuta observed and wrote about the way the Sufis lived. Imagine you are observing a friend or family member. What are some of the activities this person might participate in? Write a description of what this person might do in a typical day. For example, "After eating breakfast, _____ got her books together and went to school. After math class ..."

_____
_____
_____
_____
_____
_____
_____
_____

GROUP TOGETHER

Wouldn't it be interesting to talk with other students about what it means to be a good citizen? How do you learn about right and wrong? How are these ideas similar to or different from the values taught in Islam and Sufism? Get a few friends together and ask your teacher to help you organize a discussion group at school. Have one person take notes and another person present the group's ideas to class.

THE AFRICAN & MIDDLE EASTERN WORLD, 600–1500

WORKING WITH PRIMARY SOURCES

From *Rubaiyat*, by Omar Khayyám (about 1000)

Omar Khayyám was a mathematician and scientist from Persia. His writing is closely linked to the literature of the Sufis, who wrote poetry about humankind's intense desire to be close to God. The Sufis used poetry, dance, and music as expressions of their worship. Omar Khayyám's book of poems, Rubaiyat, is perhaps the most famous example of Sufi poetry. Several four-line verses, or quatrains, from this work are excerpted here. They focus on nature and the quickness of life's passing.

Read the following excerpt and then answer the following questions. (Notes below explain the words in bold.)

> Each **morn** a thousand Roses brings, you say;
> Yes, but where leaves the Rose of Yesterday?
> And this first Summer month that brings the Rose
> Shall take **Jamshýd** and **Kaikobád** away.
>
> A Book of Verses underneath the Bough,
> A Jug of Wine, a Loaf of Bread—and Thou
> Beside me singing in the Wilderness—
> Oh, Wilderness were Paradise **enow**!
>
> The Wordly Hope men set their Hearts upon
> Turns Ashes—or it prospers; and **anon**,
> Like Snow upon the Desert's dusty Face,
> Lighting a little hour or two—is gone.

(Notes: **morn** is a shortened version of "morning"; **Jamshýd** and **Kaikobád** are Persian kings; **enow** is a poetic way of saying "enough"; **anon** means "soon")

1. How would you answer the poet's question in the second line?

2. What does the poet mean when he says "this first Summer month . . . Shall take **Jamshýd** and **Kaikobád** away"?

3. In the second verse, the poet compares "the Wilderness" to Paradise. List the words and phrases from the pleasant scene he describes that support this comparison.

4. The third verse uses a simile of snow falling on the desert. What does this simile mean in the verse?

5. Would you say this was a happy or a sad poem? Explain your answer.

WRITE ABOUT IT

On the lines below, write your own verse about a similar subject.

34 CHAPTER 6

CHAPTER 7

HOUSES OF WISDOM: ISLAMIC ARTS AND SCIENCES

CHAPTER SUMMARY

The Muslim world made important contributions to the fields of art and science. Muslim thinkers and artists have influenced scientists and philosophers throughout history.

ACCESS

To organize the information in this chapter, copy the main idea map graphic organizer (see page 8 in this workbook) in the space below. In the center oval, write *Islamic arts and sciences*. Label each of the surrounding ovals with a category such as *astronomy*, *physics*, *mathematics*, and so forth. Add notes to each of these categories about specific advances and discoveries made in each field.

CAST OF CHARACTERS

Write a sentence explaining why each of these people was important.

Abu Jafar al-Ma'mun _____

Abu Ali Hasan Ibn al-Haitham (965–1040) _____

Abu Bakr Muhammad ar-Razi (864–930) _____

Abu Raihan al-Biruni (973–1048) _____

Abu Zayd ibn Khaldun (1332–1406) _____

Ibn Tufayl (1110–1185) _____

Ibn Rushd (1126–1198) _____

Abu Abdallah ibn Battuta (1304–1368) _____

Omar Khayyám (1048–1123) _____

WORD BANK

rihla scriptures bequeathed imposed speculated theory embarked observant

Choose words from the Word Bank to complete the sentences. One word is not used at all.

1. The _____ about how societies change explains how societies go through a cycle.
2. The ideas of the great thinkers were _____ to future generations.
3. The holy man read from the _____ of his religion.
4. If you are a scientist, it is important that you are _____.
5. The philosopher _____ on the meaning of life.
6. The traveler _____ upon her journey, or _____.

WORD PLAY

Look up in a dictionary the word that you did not use. Write a sentence using that word.

WITH A PARENT OR PARTNER

In your history journal, make a three-column chart with the headings *verb, noun,* and *adjective.* Organize the terms from the word bank according to their parts of speech. With a parent or partner, go through the chapter and add any words you don't know. Look these up in a dictionary and add them to your list.

CRITICAL THINKING
CAUSE AND EFFECT

The reason that something happens is known as a *cause*. An event or development that results from the cause is the *effect*. Writers often use signal words such as *because, so,* or *as a result* to signal a cause-and-effect relationship. Look at this example.

CAUSE	EFFECT
BECAUSE Muhammad stated the importance of the search for knowledge,	al-Ma'mun organized the House of Wisdom.

Think about the Muslim scholars and artists described in Chapter 7, and how their work affected or was affected by the work of others. Draw lines to match the "causes" in the left column with the "effects" in the right column. (There is one extra effect.)

CAUSE	EFFECT
1. BECAUSE al-Haitham studied the nature of light and studied the eye,	a. Thomas Aquinas was inspired to use logic to demonstrate the truth of the Bible.
2. BECAUSE people always seemed to sneeze in the springtime,	b. her life was saved.
3. BECAUSE Ibn Rushd made efforts to bring philosophical logic and religious faith into line with each other,	c. a theory of how societies change was developed.
	d. ar-Razi noticed that hayfever is associated with pollen.
4. BECAUSE Ibn Battuta kept such detailed accounts of his travels,	e. their way of life and tastes became a part of Spanish culture.
5. BECAUSE the character Shahrazad was able to tell such interesting stories,	f. he was the first person to provide a theory about how vision works.
6. BECAUSE Arabs and Berbers formed the ruling class in Spain,	g. it became one of the greatest contributions of the Muslims to world art.

WORKING WITH PRIMARY SOURCES

Read the poem *Three Moorish Maidens Fair* below. Then answer the following questions.

Three Moorish maidens enchanted me
in Ja-en [a Moorish town].
Aisha, Fatima, and Marien

Three Moorish maidens fair
Were going to pick olives,
[And] found the trees were bare
in Ja-en.
Aisha, Fatima, and Marien

The olives were all gone
The little maids forlorn.
Their faces lost their bloom
in Ja-en.
Aisha, Fatima, and Marien

Three Moorish maidens so fair,
Three Moorish maidens so fair,
They went to pick some pears
in Ja-en.
Aisha, Fatima, and Marien

1. Summarize what is happening in the poem.

2. Based on the pattern that the poet uses, if the poem were to continue, what do you think might happen in the next verse?

3. On the lines below, write what you think could be the next verse of the poem.

4. What elements in the poem make it easy to memorize?

HISTORY JOURNAL

Don't forget to share your history journal with your classmates, and ask if you can see what their journals look like. You might be surprised—and get some new ideas.

THE AFRICAN & MIDDLE EASTERN WORLD, 600–1500

ALL OVER THE MAP
LOCATION

Read the description of Ibn Battuta's route from his home to Mecca below. Then do the following exercises.

Ibn Battuta traveled all over the Arab world. He was born in Tangier in 1304 and began his pilgrimage to Mecca in 1325. He traveled along the northern coast of Africa through cities such as Algiers, Tunis, Tripoli, and on to Alexandria and Cairo. From Cairo, ibn Battuta and his fellow travelers continued toward the Red Sea. He traveled north to Jerusalem and then turned south and continued along the eastern side of the Red Sea, until he finally reached Mecca.

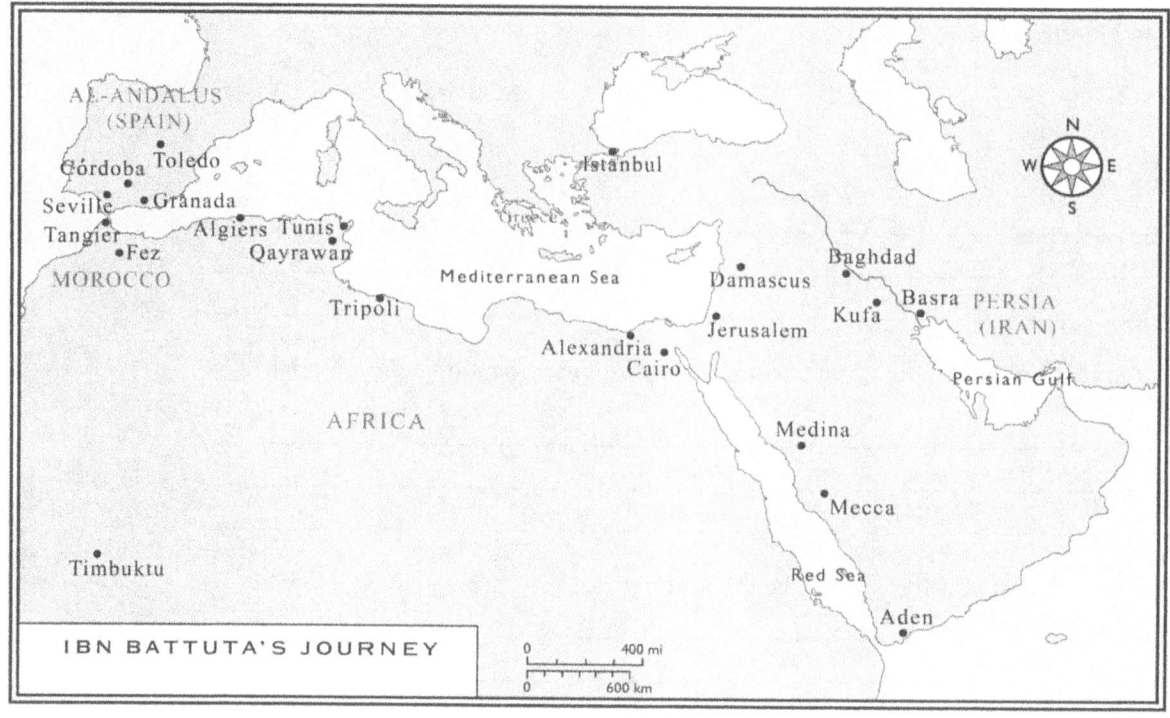

1. Circle all the cities Ibn Battuta visited.
2. Draw the route he traveled on the map.
3. Use the mileage scale to calculate the total distance of his journey, and write the answer here:

_____
_____

CHAPTER 8
NOW IT'S ISTANBUL, NOT CONSTANTINOPLE: THE OTTOMAN EMPIRE

CHAPTER SUMMARY
Ottoman leaders and their armies successfully expanded the Ottoman Empire throughout the Balkan Peninsula and to Europe.

ACCESS
Rulers of nations or people have a great impact on life during the time of their leadership. Make a two-column chart. In the first column, list all the sultans mentioned in the chapter. You can add the names as you read. Then, in the second column, write down a few facts about what happened under the rule of each of these sultans, and why each was important.

CAST OF CHARACTERS
As you read, match up each person with the correct description by writing the letter of the correct description on the line.

_____ 1. Osman
_____ 2. Orhan
_____ 3. John Comnenus
_____ 4. Sinan
_____ 5. Murad II
_____ 6. Mehmed
_____ 7. Kritovoulos
_____ 8. Selim I
_____ 9. Suleyman I
_____ 10. Khair ad-Din Barbarosa
_____ 11. Roxelana
_____ 12. Mustapha
_____ 13. Mustafa Ali
_____ 14. Abdulhemid II

a. son of Suleyman and next in line as sultan who was killed by his father because of Roxelana's lies
b. pirate-chief from Algiers who formed an alliance with Suleyman to take over parts of North Africa
c. contestant to the Byzantine throne who asked Orhan to help him win the throne
d. the last sultan of the Ottoman Empire
e. author of *Counsel for Sultans* describing the success of earlier rulers
f. governor of a province in western Anatolia and father of Orhan
g. sultan under whose leadership the Ottomans conquered Constantinople
h. son of Osman and leader of an Ottoman army that took over most of Anatolia and the Balkan Peninsula
i. a Greek governor for the Ottomans
j. sultan called *Suleyman the Magnificent* who led the Ottomans to take over most of the lands around the Mediterranean Sea and also built the Sulemaniyya Mosque
k. slave wife of Suleyman who saw to the deaths of his son and vizier
l. sultan who introduced the *devshirme*
m. sultan who defeated the Egyptians and added Egypt to the Ottoman Empire
o. architect of the sultans, who designed mosques in Istanbul

WORD BANK

sovereignty   vizier   infidels   siege

Choose words from the Word Bank to complete the paragraph. One word is not used.

The sultans wanted to expand Islamic _____. Sometimes they would lead their armies in battle and place cities under _____. Other times they would turn to their _____ for advice.

WORD PLAY

1. Look up in a dictionary the word you did not use in the exercise. Write a sentence using that word that clearly shows its meaning.

2. Look up each word from the Word Bank in the dictionary. Write as many words you can think of that have a similar meaning as each word. Then look up the word in a thesaurus to find out about any others.

WITH A PARENT OR PARTNER

Think about the word *sovereignty*. With a parent or partner, make a list in your history journal of places in the world that have *sovereignty*.

CRITICAL THINKING
FACT OR OPINION?

A fact is a statement that can be proved. An opinion is a judgment of things or people, but it cannot be proved or disproved. Read the following statements from the chapter. Write the letter "F" next to each statement that is a fact and the letter "O" next to each statement that is an opinion.

_____ 1. Osman's sultanate was crudely organized.

_____ 2. Orhan's Ottoman army had taken over most of Anatolia.

_____ 3. The Ottomans were ruthless in their takeover of the Balkan Peninsula.

_____ 4. For centuries, Constantinople's mighty stone walls had defied all takers.

_____ 5. Of course, each wife wanted to see her own son succeed as the next sultan, and Roxelana was no different.

WHAT HAPPENED WHEN?

Fill in the timeline to explain what happened on the following dates. Draw lines to connect dots and events.

1071	1258	1300	1326	1421–1451	1451
1453	1516	1520	1557	1907	1922

WORKING WITH PRIMARY SOURCES

Read the following quotations from the chapter. The first is Osman's dying words to his son, Orhan. In this passage, Osman requests that his son continue on with his mission to expand the Islamic empire. The second passage is a description of Orhan as written by Ibn Battuta. Here, Orhan is described as following his father's directions.

I.

... cultivate justice and thereby embellish the earth. Rejoice my departed soul with a beautiful series of victories ... propagate religion by thy arms.

II.

Of fortresses he possesses nearly a hundred, and for most of his time he is continually engaged in making the rounds of them. ... It is said that he has never stayed for a whole month in any town. He also fights with the infidels continually and keeps them under siege.

WRITE ABOUT IT

In your history journal, write a short essay about a time when you were asked to do something important by a parent, family member, or friend. Describe how and why you did what you were asked to do, and how you felt about it.

THE AFRICAN & MIDDLE EASTERN WORLD, 600–1500

ALL OVER THE MAP

Study the map of Ottoman Expansion. Then answer the following questions.

1. What city was a part of the Ottoman Empire in 1326?

2. What three cities in Africa were added to the Ottoman Empire by 1453?

3. Which two bodies of water did the Ottoman Empire encompass?

4. Use the mileage scale to calculate about how much farther west the Ottoman Empire expanded between 1453 and 1566. (Give distances in both miles and kilometers. To calculate kilometers, use the mileage scale or multiply the miles by 1.61.)

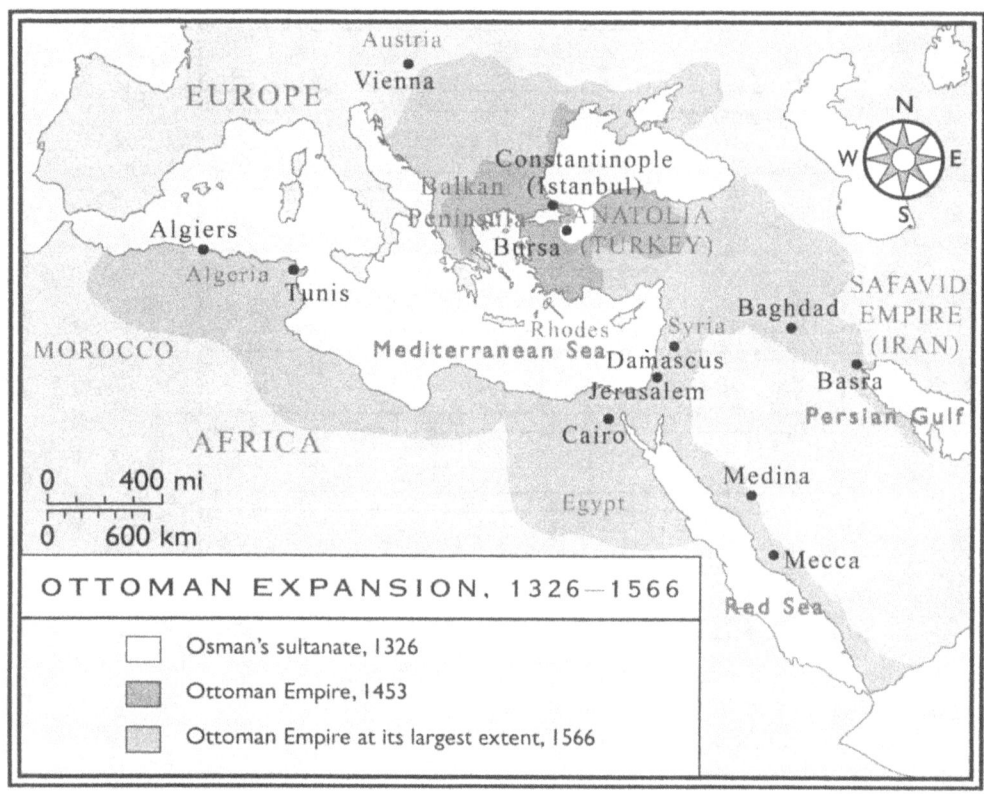

CHAPTER 9

WHERE GOLD GROWS AS CARROTS DO: GHANA AND THE AFRICAN GRASSLANDS

CHAPTER SUMMARY

The kingdom of Ghana, located in the grasslands of West Africa, prospered from trade with desert caravans. Berbers introduced Islam to the Ghana leadership, and eventually the Almoravids, a group of Sunni Muslims, converted the kingdom by force and brought about its decline.

ACCESS

This chapter discusses the enormous impact that caravan trade had on the people living in Ghana. To organize the information, make a K-W-L chart in your history journal (see page 8 of this guide). In the *K* column, write down anything you already know about West Africa (if you don't know anything, that's okay). In the *W* column, make a list of any questions you have about the chapter (for example: How did the people survive in such a hot, dry climate? What goods did they trade with the desert caravans? How did caravans contribute to the spread of ideas?). After you have finished the chapter, write down in the *L* column the answers to your questions and anything else you have learned about the kingdom of Ghana.

CAST OF CHARACTERS

Identify the people below and explain in complete sentences why each was important.

Soninke _____

Berbers _____

Abdallah ibn Yasin _____

Almoravids _____

WORD BANK

Ghana   grassland   chiefdom   jihad   millet   *ribat*   dehydration

Choose the correct word from the Word Bank to complete the sentences below.

1. People of West Africa mixed _____ with water and boiled it for a breakfast meal.

2. If caravans lost their way in the desert, all the travelers were in danger of dying from _____.

3. Devout Muslims set out to convert areas to Islam by waging _____.

4. The people of West Africa believed their _____ was a divine king.

5. The institution of the _____ helped spread Islam through West Africa and the Sahara Desert.

6. People survived in the _____ by hunting wild game, raising livestock, and harvesting wild grains.

WORD PLAY

Look up in a dictionary the word you did not use. Include this word in a sentence that clearly shows its meaning.

_____

THE AFRICAN & MIDDLE EASTERN WORLD, 600–1500

WITH A PARENT OR PARTNER

Working with a parent or partner, try to make one sentence using at least three of the words in the word bank. The sentence should express information from the chapter as well.

_____

_____

WRITE ABOUT IT

Chapter 9 starts with a description of daily life for people in the African grasslands. On page 103, it says simply, "Their lives were hard." Imagine you live in a West African village. The year is 750. In your history journal, write an account of a typical day. Describe what you eat for breakfast and how you spend the day. Do you tend livestock or work in the fields? What does your village look like? What worries or concerns do you have? In your account, use information from the chapter to show why this way of life was "hard."

CRITICAL THINKING
CAUSE AND EFFECT

The reason that something happens is called a *cause*. The thing that happens is known as the *effect*. Writers often use signal words such as *because, so,* or *as a result* to signal a cause-and-effect relationship. The chapter describes how Ghana evolved from a land of poor farmers to a powerful kingdom. To understand the different events and developments that brought about this change, match the causes with the effects in the chart below. Draw lines to match each cause in the right-hand column with each effect in the left-hand column. (There is one extra effect.)

CAUSE	EFFECT
1. Trade with desert caravans brought wealth to towns.	a. Leaders and kings made sacrifices to the gods to keep them happy.
2. People in Ghana needed salt to preserve their food in the hot climate.	b. Abdallah Ibn Yasin established a *ribat*, where people could learn to live according to strict Sunni Islamic principles.
3. People believed the gods could reward them by sending rain and allowing the crops to grow.	c. The Arabic language spread to West Africa through Muslim advisers to the king.
4. Ghana was located along the Niger River, which flowed into the desert borderlands.	d. Muslims honored the king by clapping their hands.
5. Muslim visitors brought skills to the kingdom, including reading, writing, and mathematics.	e. The Berbers moved in and forced the Soninke people of Ghana to migrate south.
6. People living in Ghana didn't have salt or cloth.	f. Towns prospered and grew into cities.
7. The Soninke people probably believed their Ghana was divine.	g. A typical Ghana would include Muslims in his circle of advisers.
8. At first, the Berbers resisted living by Islamic law.	h. The Soninke people treated their king with great reverence.
9. After the spread of Islam, the kingdom of Ghana went into a decline.	i. Traders stopped at salt deposits near oases and loaded salt on their caravans.
10. Islamic law was written in Arabic.	j. Many boat traders doing business with desert caravans passed through Ghana.
	k. People in Ghana mined gold to exchange for goods they needed but didn't have.

WORKING WITH PRIMARY SOURCES

The Book of Routes and Realms by Abu 'Ubayd 'Abd Allah bin 'Abd al-'Aziz al-Bakri (11th century)
Read the description of Ghana below and answer the questions that follow.

> The city of Ghana consists of two towns situated on a plain. One of these towns, which is inhabited by Muslims, is large and possesses twelve mosques, in one of which they assemble for the Friday prayer. . . . The king's town is six miles distant from this one and bears the name of Al Ghaba. . . . The king has a palace, a number of domed dwellings all surrounded with an enclosure like a city wall. In the king's town, and not far from his court of justice, is a mosque where the Muslims who arrive at his court pray. Around the king's town are domed buildings and groves and thickets where the sorcerers of these people, men in charge of their religious cult, live. In them too are the idols and the tombs of their kings. . . . The king's interpreters, the official in charge of his treasury, and the majority of his ministers are Muslims. Among the people who follow the king's religion, only he and his heir apparent (who is the son of his sister) may wear sewn clothes. All other people wear robes of cotton, silk, or brocade, according to their means.

COMPREHENSION

1. Where do the Muslims practice their faith?

2. Describe where the king's religious leaders live and worship.

3. Why would the king want a Muslim to be in charge of his treasury?

4. Circle or underline the words that indicate what the writer might think of the king's religion. Do you think this is a positive or negative opinion? Explain your answer.

5. By "sewn clothes," the writer means clothes that were made by sewing different parts together. The robes worn by the other people would be more like robes that they simply wrapped around themselves. Why would sewn clothes be reserved for the king and his heir, and not for anyone else?

THE AFRICAN & MIDDLE EASTERN WORLD, 600–1500

ALL OVER THE MAP
INTERACTION

Make the following changes to the map below to show trade routes in Ghana from 700 to 1200.

LEGEND
- ☐ Grasslands
- ☐ Sahara Desert
- ☐ Ghana
- ☐ Gold
- ☐ Salt deposits

GHANA, 700–1200

1. Locate and label the following cities:
   Awdaghost   Taghaza   Zawila   Qayrawan   Fez   Kumbi Saleh   Sijilmasa
2. Label these rivers: Senegal River, Niger River, Volta River; and these bodies of water: Mediterranean Sea; Atlantic Ocean
3. Use labels and shading to indicate the following regions: grasslands; the Sahara Desert; Ghana. Then key these shading patterns where indicated in the legend.
4. Locate the area where gold was mined and use an icon to identify it on the map. Key this icon in the legend.
5. Indicate with shading the general area where salt deposits were found, and key this shading in the legend.
6. Draw the route caravans probably followed to bring salt to Ghana in exchange for gold.
7. Use the mileage scale to calculate the round-trip distance of this route. Write your answer here.

_____

8. How were the rivers useful to the traders in Ghana?

_____
_____

WRITE ABOUT IT

In your history journal, write a paragraph that explains the following statement from the chapter: "All of this trade brought tremendous wealth to the towns, so much that some town grew into cities, and some cities grew into kingdoms." Use information shown on the map to support your statement.

46   CHAPTER 9

CHAPTER 10

SADDLEBAGS STUFFED WITH GOLD: THE EMPIRES OF MALI AND SONGHAY

CHAPTER SUMMARY

Two rich and powerful kingdoms, first Mali and then Songhay, emerged from Ghana starting in 1235. Although the leaders were Muslims, the people retained their traditional religious practices and beliefs in the African spirits. Internal rivalries and warfare with other nations led to Songhay's decline in the 16th century.

ACCESS

Each of the rulers described in the chapter strengthened his empire through different actions. In your history journal, make a chart with five columns and label them *Sundiata*, *Mansa Musa*, *Mansa Sulayman*, *Sonni Ali*, and *Muhammad Turé*. Under each name, list what each ruler did to make his empire strong, as well as why each ruler was important. Be sure to indicate which empire each person ruled, Mali or Songhay.

CAST OF CHARACTERS

Write several adjectives that describe each character below. Then write why you chose those adjectives.

                Adjectives   Why you chose them

Sundiata _____

_____

Mansa Musa _____

_____

Mansa Sulayman _____

_____

Qasa _____

_____

Banju _____

_____

Sonni Ali _____

_____

Muhammad Turé _____

_____

WORD BANK

1. Match the word with its definition.

    a) **alliance**   1. a condition of wealth or success

    b) **dignitaries**   2. a bond or connection between countries or groups

    c) **prominent**   3. people worthy of honor or rank

    d) **prosperity**   4. well-known

2. Choose words from the Word Bank to complete the sentences.

   a) The ruler led his strong and wealthy country during a time of _____.

   b) The _____ were welcomed with great respect at the ruler's palace.

   c) The two nations formed an _____ and agreed to defend each other in the event of war.

   d) The bustling, thriving market in Gao helped merchants became rich and _____ citizens.

WITH A PARENT OR PARTNER

Look up in the dictionary the words *dignitary*, *dignified*, and *dignity*. With a parent or partner, discuss how these words are related. Write your ideas on the lines.

_____

_____

CRITICAL THINKING
SEQUENCE OF EVENTS

Draw two sequence of events charts in your history journal (see page 9 of this study guide). Draw the first one with 5 boxes and label it *The Rise and Fall of Mali*. Copy the following events (or their corresponding numbers) into your chart in the correct order.

1. Internal rivalries and rebellious tribes such as the Mossi and Tuareg undermine the leadership of the *mansas*.
2. Gold is discovered in Buré and Bitu.
3. The Mali Empire reaches the height of its prosperity and power.
4. The gold trade in West Africa expands.
5. The cities of Jenne, Timbuktu, and Gao become wealthy trading centers.

Draw the second chart with seven boxes and label it *The Rise and Fall of Songhay*. Copy the following events (or their corresponding numbers) into your chart in the correct order.

1. Muhammad Turé consolidates power and strengthens the military.
2. Moroccan armies with superior weaponry invade the Sudan.
3. Songhay reaches the height of its prosperity and power in the region.
4. Sonni Ali takes over Gao from Mali, and later Timbuktu and Jenne.
5. Mohammad Turé expands trade with Islamic nations to the north
6. Internal rivalries weaken the Songhay leadership.
7. Songhay leaders establish successful trading cities along the Niger River.

WRITE ABOUT IT

Write a paragraph describing the reasons why empires like Mali and Songhay become powerful, and what causes them to go into decline.

WORKING WITH PRIMARY SOURCES

Read the description of the city of Djenne as written by al-Sadi.

> Jenne is one of the great markets of the Muslim world. . . . Merchants bring salt from mines of Taghaza [a desert oasis] and those with gold from the mines of Bitu meet [at Jenne]. These two marvelous mines have no equal in the entire universe. Everyone going to Jenne to trade reaps large profits and thus acquires fortunes whose amount can be known only to God. (May he be praised!) Because of this city, caravans flock to Timbuktu from all points of the horizon.

1. What are some of the items people bring to the market and where do they get these items?

2. According to al-Sadi, what happens to everyone who goes to Jenne to trade?

3. What does al-Sadi mean when he says, "caravans flock to Timbuktu from all points of the horizon"?

Now study the photograph on page 115, which shows a market in a modern city in West Africa on the Niger. Answer the following questions.

1. Describe what is going on in the picture.

2. What does the photograph show about the importance of the Niger to trade in West Africa?

3. If you could see a photograph of African trade from the 14th century, what would be different from what you see in this photograph? What would be the same?

WRITE ABOUT IT

In your history journal, write a short description of an important shopping place in your community. Is it a farmer's market or a shopping mall? What types of items are sold at this place? Where do people come from to shop there?

GROUP TOGETHER

Wouldn't it be interesting to know what other students think about the slave trade in ancient times? How does it compare to slavery in more recent centuries? Get a few friends together and ask your teacher to help you organize a discussion group at school. Have one person take notes and another person present the group's ideas to the class.

THE AFRICAN & MIDDLE EASTERN WORLD, 600–1500

ALL OVER THE MAP
REGION

Do the following exercises on the map to show the extent of the Mali and Songhay Empires.

1. Show the areas where gold was mined.
2. What rivers are near these areas? _____
3. What cities are located on the Niger River?
   _____
4. Locate and label these cities on the map.
5. Why might their location help the growth of these cities?
   _____
6. Use shading and patterns to show the Mali and Songhay Empires. Complete the map key to identify the patterns you used. Be sure to indicate which Mali territory became part of Songhay, and include this in the key.

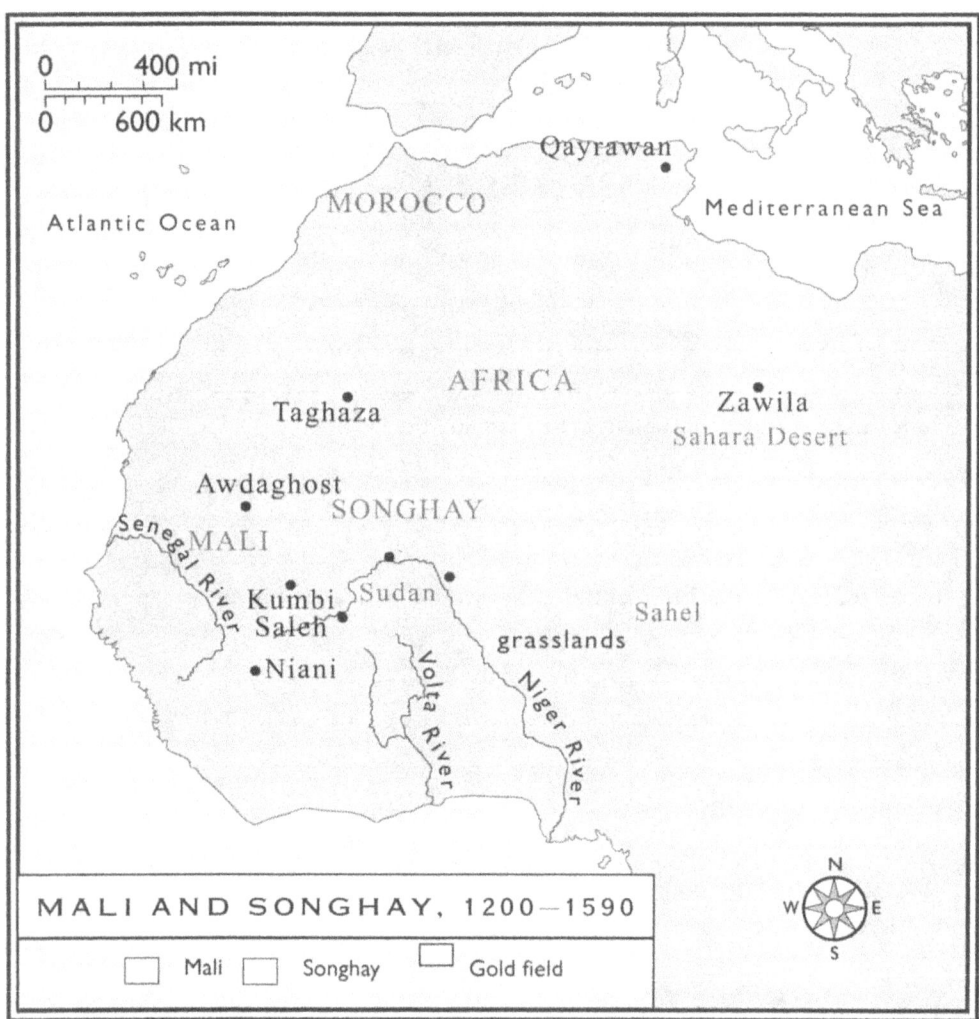

MALI AND SONGHAY, 1200—1590

CHAPTER 11
ONIS AND OBAS: THE FOREST KINGS OF WEST AFRICA

CHAPTER SUMMARY

The Yoruba people lived in and around the trading center of Ifé, where traders came with goods such as ivory and kola nuts from the forests. The Yoruba kings, called the Oni, were thought to be divine according to ancient tradition. Beautiful bronze and brass sculptures were made to honor the kings, or Obas, of neighboring Benin.

ACCESS

Think about the various ways that rulers of countries come to power. How do American politicians, for example, become presidents? Make a list of the different ways of gaining that exist today and ones that existed in the past. When you read about the Onis, Obas, and Alafins, pay special attention to the source of their power. Did you include that route to power on your list? Do rulers today gain power in the same way?

CAST OF CHARACTERS

Write a few sentences identifying each person below and explaining why he is important.

Ewuare _____
_____
_____
_____

Oguola _____
_____
_____
_____

WITH A PARENT OR PARTNER

What qualities make a great leader? Discuss this question with a parent or another partner. Use the following questions to frame your discussion.

1. Make a list of adjectives that describe such a person. Write them down in your history journal.

2. How many of these words could you apply to yourself, or to other people you know?

3. Think about leaders in power today. Can you use any of these words to describe them?

4. Which of these adjectives could you use to describe the two Obas you read about in this chapter?

5. Make a list of adjectives that mean the opposite of the adjectives on your list. Which leaders do you know about, past and present, who could be described using these words?

WORD BANK

castings   precincts   reverence   lagoons   negotiate

Choose a word from the Word Bank to complete each sentence. One word is not used.

1. These brass _____ depict famous rulers who reigned long ago.
2. Species of fish found nowhere else in the world live in these _____.
3. Learning to _____ is a skill that helps people settle disputes.
4. People came from all over the region to exchange goods in the city's _____.

WORD PLAY

Look up in a dictionary the word you did not use. On the lines below, write down its root word. List as many other words as you can that come from that root word. Look these words up in a dictionary and then explain how the meaning of these words relates to the word from the word bank. Identify the parts of speech for each word: is it a noun, verb, adjective, or adverb?

_____
_____
_____
_____

CRITICAL THINKING
MAIN IDEA AND SUPPORTING DETAILS

Sentences 1, 2, and 3 state main ideas from the chapter. Make a check mark in front of the sentences that support the main ideas.

1. Ifé was a perfect place for traders.
    a)_____ Ifé's divine king was called the Oni.
    b)_____ Ifé was considered the holy "mother-city" to all Yoruba.
    c)_____ Ifé was located between forests and grasslands and near water.
    d)_____ Ifé was on the shortest route from the forest to Jenne.

2. Most trade in Ifé was local.
    a)_____ Porters carried loads as far as 100 miles.
    b)_____ Ifé women did most of the trading.
    c)_____ The women traded things they made and fruits and vegetables they grew.
    d)_____ Ivory came from the tusks of elephants that lived in the forests.

3. Oba Ewuare fought wars of expansion.
    a)_____ Oral tradition says that Ewuare was powerful and wise.
    b)_____ Ewuare captured more than 200 towns and villages.
    c)_____ Ewuare appointed ordinary citizens to a royal council.
    d)_____ Land that Ewuare annexed added greatly to the size of the empire.

WORKING WITH PRIMARY SOURCES

Study the photograph of the terracotta head on page 131 and the brass casting of a musician on page 132. Read the captions for both. Then answer the questions below.

1. What strikes you about the art in these photographs? Describe the details and features that get your attention.

2. What does the quality of the sculpture say about the people who made it?

3. Why would a society such as the Yoruba need productive farming in order to have a large ruling class?

4. How do archaeologists know that Ifé had many craftspeople and artists?

5. What conclusions can you draw about Benin society from the brass casting of the horn blower?

WRITE ABOUT IT

Send yourself back in time. It is 1500, and you live in a tiny forest settlement in Western Africa. You are seeing Benin City for the very first time. Describe what you see, hear, smell, taste, and feel. Be sure to tell what impresses you most and why.

ALL OVER THE MAP
INTERACTION

Make the following changes to the map to show the forest kingdoms of West Africa, 1000–1500.

1. Indicate on the map, using icons, where the following products came from: gold, kola nuts, ivory, slaves. Key these icons in the legend.
2. Locate and label the following cities: Jenne, Timbukto, Gao, Ifé, Oyo, Benin
3. What do all these cities have in common?

   _____

4. Use shading or patterns to indicate tropical forest, grassland, and desert areas, and key these patterns in the legend.
5. Draw the routes on the map, using arrows to show how goods traveled from one place to another.
6. Explain the importance of the Niger River to this trade route.

   _____
   _____

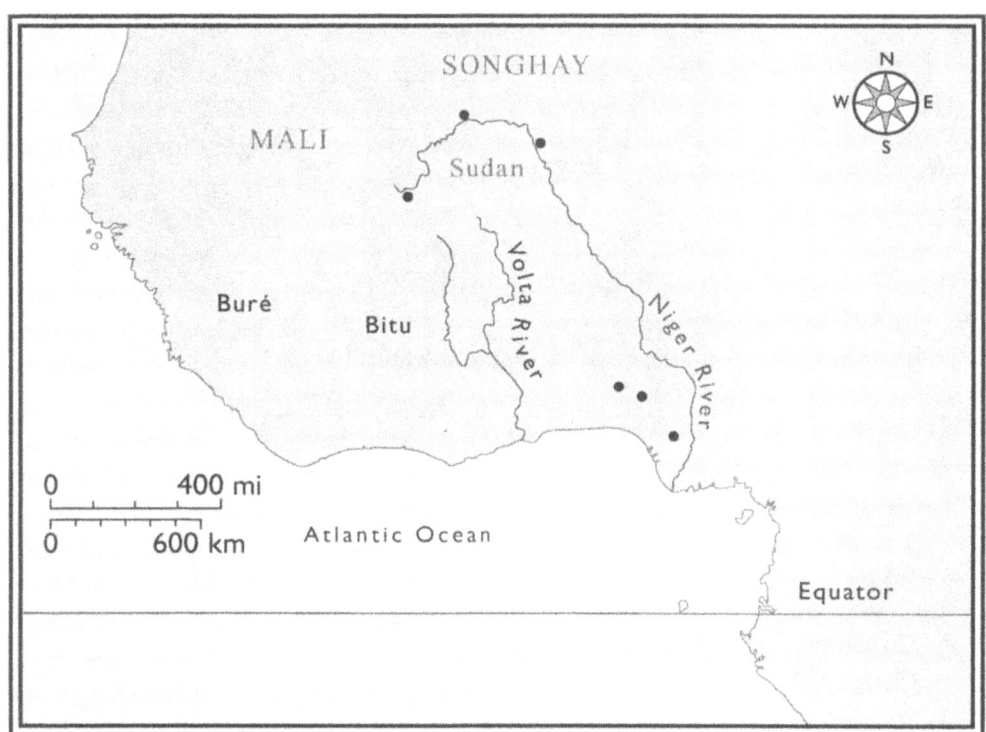

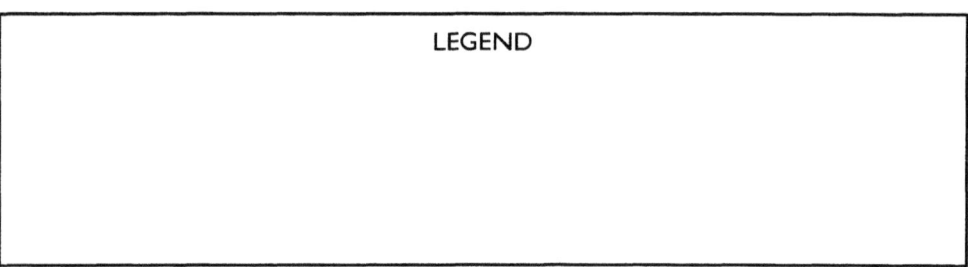

LEGEND

54 CHAPTER 11

CHAPTER 12

THERE'S TREASURE IN THOSE HILLS!: GREAT ZIMBABWE AND THE SHONA OF SOUTHERN AFRICA

CHAPTER SUMMARY

The civilizations of southeastern Africa first evolved from Bantu-speaking peoples. Over time they gave rise to the prosperous trading centers of Mapungubwe and Great Zimbabwe. After these cities went into decline, the kingdom of Mwenemutapa took over trade in the region, which was overrun by Portugal in the 1600s.

ACCESS

The chapter describes everyday life for the people who lived in the southeastern savannah of Africa. Family was very important in these villages, because family members depended on each other for survival. Think about your own family. How do you rely on each other for your basic needs? What daily needs come from the family, and what comes from outside the home? Make a list of everyone in your family, and what each member contributes to the household. Then make a list of all the things you need for your survival every day (such as food and water, housing, and so forth). Indicate on this list how these needs are provided—do they come from other family members, your community, other services?

CAST OF CHARACTERS

Write a sentence identifying and explaining the importance of each person or group of people listed below.

Bantu _____

_____

Shona _____

_____

Mutota _____

_____

Mutope _____

_____

WORD BANK

sorghum   kin   rift   kraals   coincided   prestige   disdain

Choose a word from the Word Bank to complete each sentence. One word is not used.

1. Kings wore clothes made of textiles from India to show off their _____.
2. Eventually, a _____ developed between the people who raised cattle and those who raised crops of _____.
3. Portuguese missionaries felt _____ toward the native religions of southeastern Africa.
4. The decline of trading between the Shona and Swahili people _____ with the arrival of Portuguese merchants in the 1600s.
5. The Bantu built enclosures for cattle known as _____.

THE AFRICAN & MIDDLE EASTERN WORLD, 600–1500

WORD PLAY

Look up in a dictionary the word you did not use. Then write a sentence with that word that clearly shows the word's meaning.

_____

_____

WITH A PARENT OR PARTNER

The word "stonewall" appears frequently in this chapter. It refers to the walls the Shona people built of stone. Many words are formed by combining two different words. Some examples include *sometime, cowshed, railroad*. With a parent or partner, see how many other examples you can think of. First look for these kinds of words in the chapter. Then think of other words. Make your lists separately and then read them aloud to each other.

CRITICAL THINKING
CAUSE AND EFFECT

The chapter describes several developments that took place over a long period of time. These slowly brought about changes for the people of southeastern Africa. The chart below lists these developments, or causes, in the right-hand column. The results, or effects, of these causes are listed in the left-hand column, but they are not in the correct order. Draw lines to connect each cause with its correct effect. Note that there is one extra cause.

CAUSE	EFFECT
1. The Bantu started herding cattle.	a. According to legend, Mutota abandoned Great Zimbabwe and conquered Dande, a region to the north.
2. Leaders are needed to solve disputes over land.	b. The kingdom of Mwenemutapa goes into decline as the kings lose their main source of wealth and power.
3. Gold is discovered and mined inland from the east coast.	c. The kings of Great Zimbabwe moved north, where the prosperous gold and copper trade with the coastal cities had relocated.
4. Great Zimbabwe prospers from trade with the city of Kilwa.	d. People build complex villages arranged around sturdy enclosures made of stone.
5. The dry, fragile environment around Great Zimbabwe possibly could no longer support such a large population.	e. East African chiefs show off their prestige with glass beads, cloth, and other items gained through trade with Europeans.
6. Swahili traders began traveling by the Zambezi River to do business with the Shona people, bypassing the old trading routes that passed through Great Zimbabwe.	f. A written record of court life in Karanga describes the power structure of the king's administration and family.
7. The stone walls fell into ruin over time.	g. The powerful trading empire of Karanga, also known as Mwenemutapa, dominates the Shona civilization in the 15th and 16th centuries.
8. Mutota establishes his new capital at Mwenemutapa, and his successor, Mutope, extends their power over the Shona people.	h. Villages become more organized, with chiefs as their leaders.
9. European traders come to the northern kingdom to exchange goods for gold.	i. The ruling classes of Great Zimbabwe enjoy luxuries imported from as far away as Persia and China.
10. Manuel de Faria y Sousa, a historian from Portugal, describes court traditions in the kingdom of Karanga.	j. Mapungubwe becomes a rich trading center, supplying gold, ivory, and copper to the coastal cities of Sofala and Kilwa.
11. Portugal takes over trade on the Zambezi River and imposes stiff taxes.	

WITH A PARENT OR PARTNER

Often, causes and effects are joined together in a sentence with the word *so*. When you have completed the exercise, show your work to a parent or partner. Read aloud the cause-and-effect matches, linking them with the word *so*.

WORKING WITH PRIMARY SOURCES

Hymn to Mwari (sometime after 600)

Read the following excerpt of the song of praise to Mwari, the Shona god of rain, and study the photograph of the sculpture on page 140. Then answer the following questions.

> Great Spirit!
> Piler up of rocks into towering mountains! . . .
> Caller forth of the branching trees:
> Thou bringest forth the shoots
> That they stand erect.
> Thou has filled the land with mankind . . .
> Thou givest of rain to mankind:
> We pray to thee,
> Hear us, Lord!
> Show mercy when we beseech thee, Lord.
> Thou are on high with the spirits of the great.
> Thou raisest the grass-covered hills
> Above the earth . . .

1. What phrases indicate that the Shona people believed that Mwari was a powerful being?

2. What connection does the hymn make between water and the survival of the people?

3. Why would water be important to the Shona people?

4. What does the sculpture represent?

5. Why do you think the Shona people saw a link between the animal shown in the sculpture and their beliefs about the rain god?

6. Write a paragraph explaining why this hymn would be part of an important ritual for the priests and farmers of Shonaland. Use details from the chapter to support your statements.

WRITE ABOUT IT

In your history journal, rewrite the excerpt using your own words. How would you express this poem in today's language?

THE AFRICAN & MIDDLE EASTERN WORLD, 600–1500

ALL OVER THE MAP
INTERACTION

Complete the following exercises on the map to show how trade routes changed in southeastern Africa from 1000 to 1600.

1. Locate and label these major trading centers:

   Great Zimbabwe   Sofala   Kilwa   Mapungubwe

2. Label the Zambezi River.

3. How is the Zambezi River connected to the decline of Great Zimbabwe as a trading center?

4. Use shading to indicate the Shona plateau. Key this shading in a legend.

5. Use icons to show the different areas where gold and copper were discovered and mined. Identify these icons in your legend.

6. Using a colored pencil, draw arrows on the map to show trade routes to and from Great Zimbabwe and the coastal cities mentioned in the chapter. Key this color in your legend.

7. Use a different color to show how trade routes changed by the 15th century. Key this color in your legend.

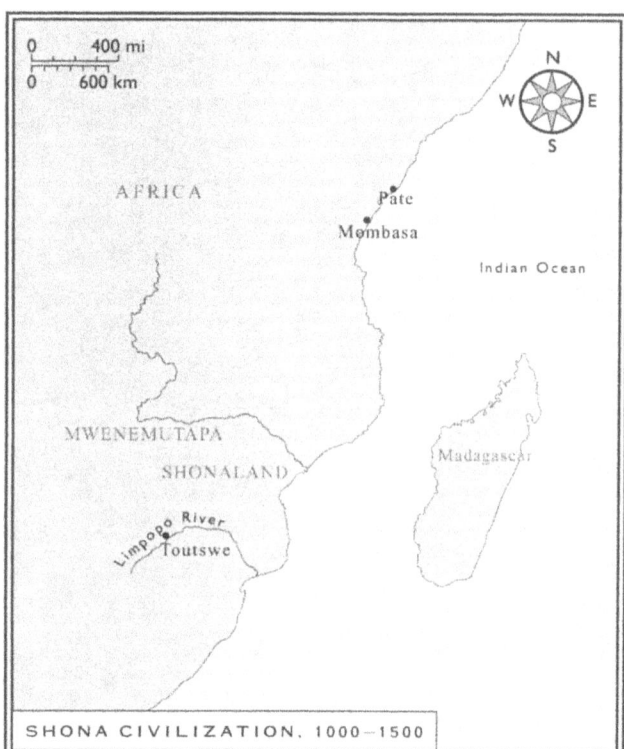

LEGEND

CHAPTER 13

THE EMPEROR'S GIRAFFE: EAST AFRICA'S SWAHILI COAST

CHAPTER SUMMARY

The Swahili people of the East African coast enjoyed a golden age from 1200 to 1500. They become part of an enormous Muslim trade network. Their city-states grew and competed. Because it controlled the gold trade, the city-state of Kilwa was the most prosperous and powerful until its collapse in the 16th century.

ACCESS

What are some of the items your city or town imports from other areas? Every city and country in today's world depends on trade every day to receive necessary goods. Long ago, trade was much simpler. As you read this chapter, compare what you know about modern-day trade with what you learn about trade on East Africa's Swahili Coast in the 15th and 16th centuries.

WITH A PARENT OR PARTNER

What are some of your favorite foods? Make a list of three fruits, vegetables, and meats that you like. Have a family member make a similar list, and then compare the two lists. Are any of the items the same? As you read the chapter, make notes on the food the Swahili people of Kilwa ate. Are any of these foods on your list? Are there any unfamiliar items? How many of them have you tried?

CAST OF CHARACTERS

Write a sentence about each person that identifies him and explains why he is important.

João de Barros _____

_____

_____

Hasan bin Sulayman _____

_____

_____

Ibn Battuta _____

_____

_____

WORD BANK

infidel   disembarked   dynasty   quay   prestigious   migrated

Choose a word from the Word Bank to complete each sentence. One word is not used.

1. Bantu people _____ to the east coast of Africa from their villages inland.
2. The _____ remained unbroken until the king lacked an heir.
3. Traders _____ at every coastal settlement to do business with local merchants.
4. There are always people at the _____ watching ships come and go.
5. Wealthy Swahili merchants showed that they were _____ by displaying precious goods from India and China to visitors.

WORD PLAY

Look up the word you did not use in a dictionary to learn the Latin word that forms its base. Then list a few other words with that same base. How many can you recall or find ion a dictionary?

_____

_____

CRITICAL THINKING
SEQUENCE OF EVENTS

The following events illustrate the rise and fall of the great city-state of Kilwa. Write the numbers of the events in their proper order in the chart below.

1. Bantu-speakers added words about marine life to their language.
2. A Yemeni clan migrated to Kilwa and established a sultanate.
3. Bantu-speakers from West Africa migrated east.
4. Kilwa is abandoned.
5. Ibn Battuta visited Kilwa.
6. The Swahili learned to mine offshore reefs for coral.

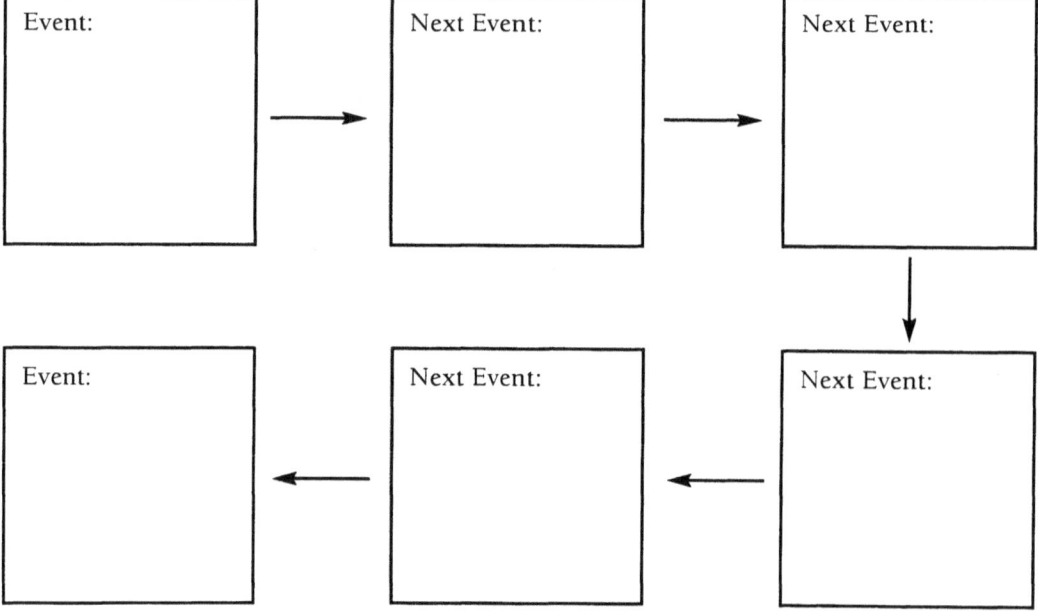

60   CHAPTER 13

WORKING WITH PRIMARY SOURCES

Read the following two excerpts that describe life and business on Mombasa, one of the great trading city-states of the East Africa coast. Then answer the questions that follow.

> We came to Mambasa [Mombasa], a large island two days' journey by sea from the Swahili country. It possesses no territory on the mainland. They have fruit trees on the island, but no cereals, which have to be brought to them from the Swahili. Their food consists chiefly of bananas and fish.
>
> —from *Travels in Asia and Africa,* by Ibn Battuta (14th century)

> Any merchant who comes to Mombasa and brings 1,000 pieces of cloth pays to the king duties of entrance for each 1,000 pieces of cloth one *mitical** of gold; and then they divide the 1,000 pieces of cloth into two halves, and the king takes one half; and the other half remains to the merchant; and whether he carries them beyond, or sells them in the city, he has to take this half to the king; and the king sends his to be sold at Sofala or Kilwa.
>
> —Diogo de Alacova, in a letter to the king of Portugal (1506)

*A *mitical* was a unit of currency in Mombasa

1. Explain the risks and benefits of living in Mombasa, based on information in the passages.

2. How did the king of Mombasa become rich from the trade that went on in his city?

3. Write a paragraph using information from the excerpts to explain this statement from the chapter: "Because of their reliance on trade, the coastal towns had to have close ties with their neighbors."

WRITE ABOUT IT

Imagine you are a reporter conducting an interview with Ibn Battuta. He has just returned from a visit to Kilwa. What would you most want to know about the powerful city-state? Write three questions. Then imagine Ibn Battuta's answers, based on what you have learned about Kilwa in this chapter.

HISTORY JOURNAL

Don't forget to share your history journal with your classmates, and ask if you can see what their journals look like. You might be surprised—and get some new ideas.

THE AFRICAN & MIDDLE EASTERN WORLD, 600–1500

ALL OVER THE MAP

Directions

Use the map to help you answer the questions.

1. Compare the exports of the Swahili coast of East Africa with those of Arabia, Persia, and India. What generalization can you make about the difference between the two groups of exports?

2. What was one reason most gold was traded through Kilwa?

3. What can you assume about places that export wool and leather? Wood and pitch?

4. Explain why so many trade routes go around the coastlines. Were these routes shorter or longer than going by land?

5. How were goods transported for the overland routes across the Sahara and from Asia?

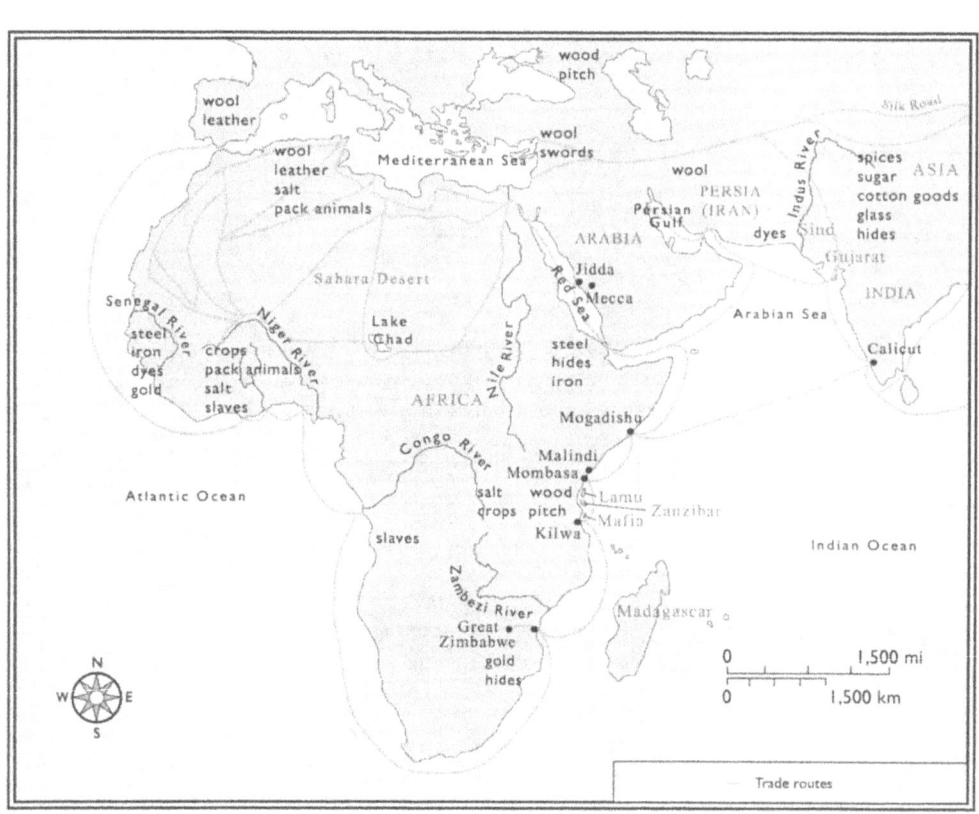

NAME

LIBRARY/ MEDIA CENTER RESEARCH LOG

DUE DATE

What I Need to Find

I need to use:
- ☐ primary sources.
- ☐ secondary

Places I **Know** to Look

Brainstorm: Other Sources and Places to Look

WHAT I FOUND

Title/Author/Location (call # or URL)

	Primary Source	Secondary Source	Suggestion	Library Catalog	Browsing	Internet Search	Web link	Book/Periodical	Website	Other	**Rate each source from 1 (low) to 4 (high) in the categories below** helpful / relevant
				How I Found it							

_____ _____
☐ ☐ ☐ ☐ ☐ ☐ ☐ ☐ ☐ ☐
☐ ☐ ☐ ☐ ☐ ☐ ☐ ☐ ☐ ☐ _____ _____
☐ ☐ ☐ ☐ ☐ ☐ ☐ ☐ ☐ ☐ _____ _____
☐ ☐ ☐ ☐ ☐ ☐ ☐ ☐ ☐ ☐ _____ _____
☐ ☐ ☐ ☐ ☐ ☐ ☐ ☐ ☐ ☐ _____ _____
☐ ☐ ☐ ☐ ☐ ☐ ☐ ☐ ☐ ☐ _____ _____

NAME _____   LIBRARY / MEDIA CENTER RESEARCH LOG   DUE DATE _____

What I Need to Find

Places I **Know** to Look

Brainstorm: Other Sources and Places to Look

I need to use:
☐ primary
☐ secondary
sources.

WHAT I FOUND

Title/Author/Location (call # or URL)

	How I Found it						Rate each source from 1 (low) to 4 (high) in the categories below	
	Suggestion	Library Catalog	Browsing	Internet Search	Web link	Primary Source / Secondary Source	helpful	relevant

☐ Book/Periodical ☐ Website ☐ Other

www.ingramcontent.com/pod-product-compliance
Lightning Source LLC
LaVergne TN
LVHW080251260326
834688LV00042BA/1216